NEW STUDIES IN ETHICS

CONTEMPORARY MORAL
PHILOSOPHY

First published May 1967
Reprinted December 1967

Published by
MACMILLAN & CO LTD
Little Essex Street London WC 2
and also at Bombay Calcutta and Madras
Macmillan South Africa (Publishers) Pty Ltd Johannesburg
The Macmillan Company of Australia Pty Ltd Melbourne
The Macmillan Company of Canada Ltd Toronto
St Martin's Press Inc New York

Library of Congress catalog card no. 67–11398

Printed in Great Britain
by Richard Clay (The Chaucer Press), Ltd., Bungay, Suffolk

Contemporary
Moral Philosophy

G. J. WARNOCK, M.A.
Fellow of Magdalen College, Oxford

MACMILLAN
London · Melbourne · Toronto

ST MARTIN'S PRESS
New York
1967

CONTENTS

EDITOR'S PREFACE

New Studies in Ethics is a series of monographs by modern philosophers, drawn from universities in Great Britain, the United States, and Australia.

Each author was asked to prepare a comprehensive and critical discussion of the views of a philosopher, or school of philosophers, influential in the history of ethical theory. As a whole, the series covers the main types of theory from the early Greeks to the present day.

In recent years a good deal has been written by analytical philosophers concerning moral discourse. What are the defining characteristics of a moral judgment? How does the evaluation of a man's character as good, or of his actions as morally right, differ logically from any factual description which could be given of him or his behaviour? These are the kinds of question with which British moral philosophers and others have been concerned for more than half a century.

With characteristic lucidity, Mr. Warnock traces the course of this debate, guiding the reader through its main stages — from the intuitionism of G. E. Moore, through the emotivism of the logical positivists and the prescriptivism of such writers as R. M. Hare to the current reconsideration of naturalism.

His clear expositions of these modern authors will be invaluable to the reader who comes new to moral philosophy; and his penetrating criticisms will be of interest to all those who are concerned to understand moral discourse.

W. D. HUDSON

I. INTRODUCTION

The aim of this essay is to provide a compendious survey of moral philosophy in English since about the beginning of the present century. Fortunately, the tale that thus falls to be told is not in outline excessively complex, and can be seen as a quite intelligible sequence of distinguishable episodes. The major stages on the road are three in number. There is, first, Intuitionism, to be considered here as represented by G. E. Moore (*Principia Ethica*, 1903), H. A. Prichard (*Moral Obligation*, published posthumously in 1949), and W. D. Ross (*The Right and the Good*, 1930, and *Foundations of Ethics*, 1939). Second, in somewhat violent reaction to the undoubted shortcomings of that style of ethics, we have Emotivism; and here the chief spokesman is C. L. Stevenson (*Ethics and Language*, 1944). And third, as an amendment of and an advance from Emotivism, we shall consider what may be called, and often is called, Prescriptivism, whose most lucid, persuasive, and original exponent is R. M. Hare (*The Language of Morals*, 1952, and *Freedom and Reason*, 1963). Other authors and other works, of course, will be mentioned in their places; but the main plot is determined by these three doctrines and their leading advocates.

It will be found that my critical discussions of the major doctrines to be surveyed are (I fear) somewhat uniformly hostile; and I have brought in, in the later pages of my essay, perhaps more controversial matter than would ordinarily be looked for in a mainly expository review. But I would defend this, if I had to, as lying in the nature of the case. For the case is, I believe, that the successive orthodoxies of moral philosophy in English in the present century have been, notwithstanding the often admirable acumen of their authors, remarkably barren. Certain questions about the nature and the basis of moral judgment which have been regarded, at least in the past, as centrally important have not only not been examined in recent theories; those theories have seemed deliberately to hold that, on those questions, there is nothing whatever that can usefully be said. There seems to have occurred an extraordinary narrowing of the field; moral philosophy has been made to look, if not simple, yet bald and jejune and, in its fruits, unrewarding. But the subject is not necessarily, I believe, so lifeless as it has been made to look; and if room is to be made for future infusions of new life, it seems essential that recent inhibiting orthodoxies should now be somewhat roughly — not, I hope, rudely — handled.

It is possible, and may be helpful, to sketch out in advance one short version of the way in which things seem to me to have gone wrong. Intuitionism, to begin with, emptied moral theory of all content by making the whole topic undiscussably *sui generis*. Fundamental moral terms were said simply to be indefinable, and fundamental moral judgments to be simply, transparently and not further explicably, self-evident. Moral truths were, it seemed, such that nothing could possibly be said about what they meant, what their grounds were, or even why they mattered at all. Now this, we may say, understandably provoked the emotivist to look quite elsewhere in search of something to be said. In effect he abandoned altogether the idea — the apparently barren idea — that moral utterances should be regarded as genuine judgments having (or even not having) statable meanings and discoverable grounds, and turned instead to the quite new topic of such utterances' *effects*. But thus, though for new reasons, the emotivist like his predecessor had nothing to say on what moral judgments are, or say, or mean; he was interested only, and somewhat crudely, in what they are *for*. Prescriptivism next contributed a meritorious distinction. We should consider, it was urged, not what is sought to be achieved *by* issuing a moral utterance, but rather what is actually done *in* issuing it — not what effect is aimed at, but what 'speech-act' is performed. This was all to the good. But this enquiry, it will be observed, still stopped short of considering what such utterances actually say, what they mean, what sort of grounds can be urged for or against them. And thus there remains out of view, or at least at the margin of attention, all that is of distinctively moral interest. For neither the 'per-locutionary' acts studied by the emotivist, nor the 'illocutionary' acts on to which prescriptivism fastens, are in any way distinctive of or peculiar to moral discourse.[1] The 'locutions' of moral discourse have a better claim to be distinctive of it; but these have yet to be rescued from the protracted neglect which seemed, indeed, merited by the ingenious vacuities of the Intuitionists, and which was continued in their successors' preoccupation with other things. There are other matters too which, one may hope, will come more clearly into view, if attention can be directed at least more nearly to the centre of the field of investigation.

That said, I would wish at once to discourage the hopes of possible unwelcome allies. Some who have been struck by the thinness of recent academic moral theory have laid the blame undiscriminatingly at the door of 'linguistic philosophy', and have seemed to adopt the notion of thickening the diet by the means, no doubt effective in their way, of confusing all the issues. This is, to say the least, unnecessary. It is not in the nature of 'linguistic philosophy' that it should find nothing much to say in moral theory. That this has been so, so far as it has been so, looks more like an aberration, and one for which the remedy consists in getting many things clearer, not everything more confused. This essay is much too short to do much in that way. The most I would hope for is that it may draw attention to some of the things that now might usefully be done. My argument, I fear, becomes increasingly congested as it proceeds, from the attempt, particularly in section V, to introduce large issues in a very few words. Those paragraphs leave everything to be said, but I hope they may be found to be, in a good sense as well as in a bad one, provoking.

II. INTUITIONISM

(i) G. E. MOORE

Consideration of intuitionism in the moral philosophy of this century starts naturally from the work of G. E. Moore. Moore, a philosopher of most distinguished ability and very great importance in the history of the subject, was by no means at his best in the field of ethics; nevertheless his *Principia Ethica* is a good deal more interesting than most intuitionist contributions, and was in fact the most widely influential of any.

We must first ask: was Moore really an intuitionist at all? For in the preface to *Principia Ethica* he goes out of his way to 'beg it may be noticed that I am not an "Intuitionist" in the ordinary sense of the term'. The ordinary intuitionist holds, according to Moore, that moral truths of many different kinds, perhaps of all kinds, may be known to be true 'by intuition' — that is, that they are, if properly considered, simply self-evident, or just seen (though no doubt not literally *seen*) to be true. Moore disagrees with this. In his view, only a small and very special class of moral judgments consists of truths which are thus self-evident; the truth of many more must be investigated by other means, and indeed can seldom, if ever, be established with certainty. It transpires, however, that in Moore's opinion all moral judgments which do not belong to, must in the end inevitably be founded upon, that special class of moral judgments which *are* self-evident; and it is, one may think, philosophically much more significant that he should hold the fundamental truths of morals to be self-evident, than that he should hold that many propositions of morals are not. Again, while it is true that Moore does not much like, and seldom employs, the term 'intuition', he sees that those who have spoken of certain truths as being known 'by intuition' have often meant by this simply that those truths are self-evident, or are known directly, without proof or argument: and in this

4

sense he himself undoubtedly maintains that the fundamental truths of morals are known 'by intuition', or alternatively, as he sometimes puts it, are Intuitions. He offers, certainly, no alternative expression of his own: and since he agrees so closely in substance with other Intuitionists, it is proper enough that his position should accept the name.

At the outset of his argument Moore expresses the well-justified conviction that much moral philosophy and some ordinary moral judgment have been persistently distorted and befogged by sheer confusion; and much of his book is devoted to pointing out, at times with a rather unpleasing and even arrogant self-assurance, the confusions in which other philosophers have so copiously indulged. His aim in so doing, and in setting out by contrast what he takes to be the true 'fundamental principles of ethical reasoning', is to advance the cause of correct moral judgment — to help his reader, that is, to see or to discover which moral propositions are actually true. Most of his argument, however, is directed to establishing the *nature* of moral propositions; and it is with his views on this matter, rather than on the question which such propositions are actually true, that we shall here be concerned.

Fortunately it is possible to summarise quite briefly what Moore takes to be the main, most persistent, and most damaging, confusion into which so many of his predecessors have fallen; and it is in his criticism of this that his own view can most readily be made clear. Ethics, Moore says, is concerned with, and may even be defined by its characteristic concern with, the predicate 'good' and its converse 'bad'; and though this concern may take more than one form, the central question is what the predicate 'good' means, or stands for. (It may be noted, and perhaps regretted, that the predicate 'bad' very quickly drops out of the argument.) This question what 'good' means, Moore insists, is not a verbal one; it would be beside the point, even if it were possible, to excogitate some synonymous expression conforming with the use made of the word 'good' by those who speak English. The real question is: what is the property for which 'good' stands? What is the property which any subject has, in virtue of which it would be true to say that that subject is good?

Now most moral philosophers, in Moore's view, though more or less aware that this was the question centrally at issue, have made some variant of a single blunder in seeking to answer it. They have tended, whether deliberately or inadvertently, to pick out some other property which some good things have, and simply to identify this other property with goodness; they have, in a peculiar but particularly important sense, *defined* goodness as just being, or being strictly dentical with, some other property. For instance, philosophers have identified goodness with the properties of being pleasant, or highly evolved, or conducive to 'self-realisation' — widely different doctrines, no doubt, but all alike mistaken, and mistaken in the same way. For — as we read on the title-page of Moore's book — 'everything is what it is, and not another thing'; but these doctrines all allege that goodness *is* some property which, as a matter of fact, it is not.

Nor is it only, Moore holds, that those views are mistaken; any view of that kind must be mistaken in just the same way. For the predicate 'good' is, in the important sense, indefinable; goodness, that is, is a simple, unanalysable, wholly non-complex property, so that there is *nothing* — and in particular no complex of parts — with which it can be rightly identified (except itself). 'If I am asked "What is good?" my answer is that good is good, and that is the end of the matter. Or if I am asked "How is good to be defined?" my answer is that it cannot be defined, and that is all I have to say about it.'[2]

Why does Moore say this? His argument is that, if 'good' were (in his sense) definable, then it would be *analytic*, or tautologous, that certain things are good: if being good were identical with being P (where P is any adjectival expression other than 'good'), then 'What is P is good' would be analytic, true by definition, and 'What is P is not good' would be self-contradictory. But it is obvious, Moore thinks, that this is never the case. For however, he holds, any object may be described — whatever predicates (other than 'good') may be truly ascribed to it — it clearly remains a further question whether that object is good: to assert that the object so described is good is always a further assertion of substance, never a mere tautology, and to deny that it is good is, even if obviously false, never self-contradictory. If this is so, it follows that 'good' is, in Moore's sense, indefinable; and it follows from that, in his view, that goodness is a simple, unanalysable quality.

We should add that goodness is also, in Moore's view, a *non-natural* quality, and that, while he regards as grossly mistaken any view whatever which attempts a definition of goodness, he regards with peculiarly withering contempt any view which identifies goodness with 'natural' qualities and so commits what he calls 'the Naturalistic Fallacy'. About this feature of Moore's position there is, however, not much to be said: for although the naturalistic fallacy has played an important and colourful part in more recent writings, in Moore's book it amounts only to the bald assertion that the quality of goodness is *not* as other qualities are — that, in particular, its presence is not to be detected by any ordinary species of observation, experience, or investigation. How is it detected, then? Some would say: by intuition. Moore does not much like this answer, probably because he rightly feels that it is not really an answer at all, but a confession of bewilderment got up to look like an answer. However, he has no other answer to give; and so the import of the term 'non-natural' remains obscure.

Moore's views about 'right' — and about 'duty' and 'obligation', which he does not sharply distinguish from 'right' — are very different from his views about 'good'. Rightness, he thinks, *is* definable; namely, it is definable in terms of goodness. For in any situation the right course of action for any agent to adopt is, by definition, that course of action which will, as a matter of fact, produce the greatest amount of good possible in the circumstances. It is clear at once, then, that on Moore's view there is a vast difference of principle between questions about what is right, and about what is good. In the latter case there is no reasoning to be done, no evidence to be assembled, no investigation to be carried out: all we can do is attend very carefully to that about which the question 'Is it good?' is asked, mentally isolating it so far as possible from other things, and carefully discriminating its several properties one from another: then we shall

7

simply see (though of course not literally *see*) that it has the property of goodness or, alternatively, that it has not. With the question 'Is this action right?', on the other hand, the case is very different. For to answer this question we should have to establish, first, what would in fact be the total consequences of performing this action; second, what would be the respective total consequences of all other courses of action open to the agent; and third, which of these alternative sets of total consequences embodied the most good — or more strictly, the most favourable surplus of good over bad.

It is a curious incidental reflection that this position as a whole, while highly anarchic in one way, is strongly conservative in another. Questions about what is good are firmly handed over, without any reference to reasons, experience, authority, or even thought, to the personal 'intuition' of each individual. Moore, however, partly as a result of heavily exaggerating the difficulty of determining what the consequences of our actions will be, is so pessimistic as to our chances of correctly ascertaining what is right that he recommends, in most cases, simple adherence to the prevalent conventions of one's society.[3] It may be guessed that those members of 'Bloomsbury' who have claimed, so surprisingly, to have been vastly influenced and illuminated by *Principia Ethica* were struck more forcibly by the first point than by the second.[4]

Moore's position, then, whatever its merits or demerits may be (to that question we shall turn in a moment) has at any rate the charm, such as it is, of the very starkest simplicity. All moral problems, on this view, have ultimately to do with the possession or non-possession by this or by that of just one quality, goodness. (We too may neglect here the unfortunate, much-neglected property of badness.) Since this is an absolutely simple property, distinguishable from and indeed independent of anything else, we have nothing to do but to 'intuit' its presence or absence; and in fact Moore holds, as we have seen, that to the discriminatingly intuitive eye its presence or absence is simply self-evident. Besides this there is only one kind of problem in morals, and that is the purely causal or factual problem what courses of action will produce as much good as possible — that is, are right. In view of Moore's announced concern with 'the fundamental principles of ethical reasoning', it is curious that his conclusion is really that there are no such principles. For on questions about goodness he has no place for reasoning at all, while on questions of what is right there is purely causal or inductive enquiry into the consequences of actions, of a kind that we might engage in without any moral interest whatever.

(ii) PRICHARD AND ROSS

Other intuitionists, among whom were conspicuous H. A. Prichard and Sir David Ross, somewhat modified the bald simplicity of Moore's doctrine, while not fundamentally or in principle dissenting from it. (So did Moore himself, in fact, in his later and slighter book *Ethics* [1912].) They wanted at least two indefinables, not one, and to make 'intuition' do more work than Moore had assigned to it.

Consider, for instance, Prichard's argument in his celebrated paper 'Does Moral Philosophy Rest on a Mistake?'[5] He suggests that in fact it does, for the following reason. We are, he says, often inclined to ask — and in this inclination, indeed, is the genesis of most moral philosophy — whether some action which we think to be our duty, or are told is our duty, really is our duty: or we ask of the same action, slightly differently, why we should do it. Now many moral philosophers, Prichard rightly supposes, have sought to offer reasons to such an enquirer as this. They have sought to offer arguments to prove that some action which he thinks to be his duty really is his duty, that he is not mistaken in thinking so; also, or alternatively, they have tried to show him what the reasons are why he should act in that way. But Prichard now suggests, very much in the manner of Moore, that all attempts of this kind are in principle misconceived. There is no reason why some action which is my duty is my duty, except precisely that it is my duty; similarly there is no reason, except that it is my duty, why I ought to do it. Consequently, if one mentions some other feature that the action may have, such as being productive of good or conducive to happiness, one is simply talking off the point. For even if the action in question be productive of good, it is not that wherein its being my duty consists; and even if it will conduce to my own or to the general happiness, that is not why I ought to do it. If someone asks of some action, then, 'Is this action my duty?', there is nothing whatever to be done along the lines of argument; it is irrelevant to consider the results of the action in the way of good or of happiness, or to offer the enquirer grounds for acting or inducements to act in that way; one can only tell him to consider, as clearly and carefully as he can, what the action is, and he will then 'see' that the action is his duty or, alternatively, is not. In order to free ourselves from the insidious and misguided inclination to look for arguments we must realise, Prichard says, 'the self-evidence of our obligations, i.e. the immediacy of our apprehension of them. . . . Or, to put the matter generally, if we do doubt whether there is really an obligation to originate A in a situation B, the remedy lies not in any process of general thinking, but in getting face to face with a particular instance of the situation B, and then directly appreciating the obligation to originate A in that situation.'[6]

In later writings Prichard greatly elaborates upon, but does not really modify, the bleak austerity of this position. He came to think, indeed, that 'obligatoriness' is not a character of actions. For what I have an obligation to do is necessarily some action which I have not yet done — which, in that sense, does not exist; but what does not exist cannot have, and cannot possibly, in Prichard's view, even be thought to have, any characters at all. My having an obligation, therefore, must be a character of something else which does exist, and is in fact, Prichard holds, a character of me, the prospective agent. However, he still holds that there is nothing much to be said about this character; it is '*sui generis*, i.e. unique, and therefore incapable of having its nature expressed in terms of the nature of anything else' (*Moral Obligation*, 1937). Thus moral philosophy seems still to be, as he had said in 1912, 'not extensive'. It consists partly, and no doubt most lengthily, in refutation of views which seek to 'reduce' goodness or obligation to things other than themselves, and apart from that in simple recognition that those attributes are *sui generis* and immediately apprehended. There seems to be no room, on this view, even for the kind of reasoning which Moore had envisaged; for whereas Moore had held that the rightness of an action consisted in its producing the greatest possible good, Prichard holds that rightness is *sui generis* exactly as goodness is and, like goodness on Moore's view, is simply evident to the discriminatingly intuitive eye.

In the writings of W. D. Ross the intuitionist position appears as somewhat etiolated indeed, but also less fanatical. There are in particular two respects in which Ross deviates in the direction of good sense. In the first place, he is unable to swallow without qualification Prichard's doctrine of 'the self-evidence of our obligations'. Perhaps he felt that it was simply too unplausible to contend that the answer to the question, what it is our duty to do, must always be self-evident; but the consideration he chiefly dwells on is this. It is, he thinks, actions of certain *kinds* whose rightness is 'immediately apprehended' — for example, of promise-keeping, or of paying a debt. But there seems to be no kind of action of which we can say without qualification that, whenever it is open to me to perform a particular action of that kind, it is my duty to do so; for, for any two kinds of action both thus asserted to be my duty, circumstances may arise, or may at any rate be imagined, in which I could perform an action of the one kind only by omitting to perform an action of the other kind. I may be confronted with a 'conflict of duties'; and in such a case, since I *can* perform only one of those actions, it cannot be held that it is my duty to do both — nor that, as Prichard seems optimistically to have supposed, it will be immediately obvious which it is my duty to do. Hence we can hold only that actions of certain general kinds are self-evidently, are intuited as being, '*prima facie* duties' — actions, that is, which it is a duty to perform *unless* that obligation conflicts with, and is over-borne by, some other.[7]

Secondly, Ross was fully conscious of a very strange, though unstressed, implication in Moore's doctrine, and to some degree also in Prichard's. If it is insisted that goodness and rightness are simple, *sui generis*, directly intuited properties, then it must seem that the question whether something is good or right is, purely and simply, the question whether it possesses one or the other of those properties; and it may seem that any consideration of its other properties would be simply irrelevant. But this is surely unacceptable. Let us agree that the goodness of a thing is not to be identified with any of its other properties, and that the rightness of an action does not simply consist in its being an action of a certain describable kind: must it not be allowed nevertheless that the goodness of a thing somehow *depends on* its possession of certain other properties, that there are other features of the action which *make* it a right action? Goodness and rightness, then, according to Ross, though intuitable, must be regarded as 'dependent' or 'consequential' properties; they are not, as it were, stuck on objects or actions like postage stamps, quite indifferently to any other features of those objects or actions, nor are other properties quite irrelevant to goodness and rightness.

These two amendments, one may say, make some attempt to rescue for moral discussion some kind of subject-matter. For if all that is self-evident is that some action is my duty *prima facie*, there is room for uncertainty and debate as to whether or not it really is my duty *sans phrase*; and even if the goodness of something is self-evident, directly intuited, it may still be made a question on what its goodness depends. It must be confessed that Ross's writings do not throw any light on how such questions are to be answered; but it is all to the good that he should recognise, and even stress, that there exists at least the possibility of asking them.

(iii) INTUITIONISM CONSIDERED

We turn now to appraisal. What — to save time by begging one or two questions — was really wrong with Intuitionism as a theory of morals? Not, I think, that much of what its proponents maintained was untrue: indeed, when allowance is made for certain eccentricities of expression, they often delineated the surface of the subject with commendable accuracy. It is rather that the theory, appraised as a contribution to philosophy, seems deliberately, almost perversely, to answer no questions, to throw no light on any problem. One might almost say that the doctrine actually consists in a protracted denial that there is anything of the slightest interest to be said. The effect of this is worse than unhelpful: it is positively misleading.

There is, we may admit, a single grain of truth which all intuitionists grasped, and characteristically dwelt upon — the truth that moral judgments are in some important way *different* from, say, assertions of empirical fact, or commands, or aesthetic judgments, or expressions of taste. Moral judgments, they rightly insisted, cannot be identified with, 'reduced to', or analysed in terms of, any of these other things; they are *different* from these things. But their account of the differences is so jejune as to be worse than useless.

It appears to have been assumed by intuitionist philosophers that it is, in general, the business of an adjective to designate a quality, a property, or a character; or at any rate, if they would not have subscribed to this general view without qualification, they did not question that it was true of the adjectives 'good' and 'right'. Thus, from the fact that goodness was felt not to be identifiable with any ordinarily discernible property of things that are good, Moore concluded merely that 'good' must designate some *other* property; Prichard, finding that 'obligatory' did not mean the same as 'expedient', or 'desirable', or 'productive of good', inferred that 'obligatory' must stand for some *other* character. On this view what distinguishes moral judgments from other things is simply that such judgments ascribe to things *different properties*, characters which are *sui generis* to moral judgment: the difference is simply a difference of subject-matter; moral judgments attribute moral qualities, and that is all there is to it.

It might be thought, with some justice, that what is wrong with this is that, while insisting that there is a difference, it amounts in practice to a refusal to discuss what the difference is. We wish to know what moral goodness is, or what it is for an action to be obligatory, and we are not told; for the 'qualities', we are told, are indefinable. But this answer is not merely dusty, ungratifying to curiosity: it is also positively misleading in a number of respects.

There is a sense, first of all, in which it can be said to exaggerate the difference of moral judgment from other things. On Moore's showing, the fact that some item is morally good appears to be, not merely different from any other fact about it, but quite unconnected with, independent of, any other fact; for all that he says, the simple *sui generis* quality of goodness might quite well be detected as attaching to anything whatever — alighting, so to speak, inexplicably and at random upon anything, of whatever kind. For Prichard there is no reason *why* what is right is right; so, for Moore, there is no reason why what is good is good — that it *is* good is not only a distinguishable, but a totally isolated, fact about it, not just different from, but unrelated to, anything else. But if so, then it seems that morality is not only not reducible to, or identifiable with, any ordinary features of the world or of human beings; it seems to stand in absolutely no relation to any such features, and to be, in the strictest sense, entirely inexplicable. The picture presented is that of a realm of moral qualities, *sui generis* and indefinable, floating, as it were, quite free from anything else whatever, but cropping up here and there, quite contingently and for no reason, in bare conjunction with more ordinary features of the everyday world. Ross, as we have noted, was certainly aware of some deficiency here; while not denying that moral rightness and goodness were distinct 'characters' of right and good things, he asserted that these characters 'depended on' other characters, that there were features of things that somehow *made* them right, or good. But he did not do more than assert that this was so: he did not explain what this puzzling kind of dependence of some 'characters' on others might be. Though he recognised the point, he cast no light upon it.

But if the intuitionist account of the distinctness of moral judgment overstates the case in this way, it seriously understates it in others. On this account the propositions of morals differ solely, though indeed completely, from others in subject-matter; they are truths (or falsehoods) on a peculiar topic, but of a quite familiar kind. To say that daffodils are yellow is to attribute a 'character' to daffodils; to say that aesthetic enjoyment is good is to attribute a 'character' to aesthetic enjoyment. But we detect the character of daffodils by looking at them: how do we detect that other character in aesthetic enjoyment? If disputes should arise, in what way might they be resolved? If I wonder whether some moral proposition is really true, how should I investigate the question, where should I look for assurance? There are, it appears, moral facts: how, then, are moral facts established? To such questions as these the theory offers, in effect, no answer at all. For to say that moral facts are recognised 'by intuition' is in part to say, unhelpfully, that such facts are *not* recognised or established in any ordinary way, and in part to offer the optimistic (and obviously false) suggestion that there is really no room here for doubt, or argument, or disagreement at all. Presumably we are to conclude that what Prichard calls 'our moral capacities of thinking' are themselves, as moral 'characters' are, *sui generis* and indefinable — that is, in effect, that on the whole question of moral argument and moral disagreement there is nothing whatever to be said, unless perhaps that they are what they are.

Finally, we must mention that deficiency in intuitionism of which later writers, as we shall find, have been most acutely conscious. Moral predicates, it was assumed, stand for moral properties. If so, to attribute a moral predicate to some subject is simply to assert that the item referred to has some moral property — it is to state that fact, to convey that piece of information. Now we have already seen that the theory leaves it, at best, unclear how pieces of moral information are related to any other features of the world, and rather more than unclear how their truth can be established or confirmed. We must now take note that it is also left very far from clear what such pieces of information, even if recognised to be true, have to do with our conduct. Let us concede that there are, here and there in the world, some items which have the moral properties intuitionists talk about, and some which have not: why should we care? Why does the presence or absence of these properties matter? In becoming aware that some proposed course of action is, say, obligatory, I have, on this theory, added to my information, I have come to know a truth about the world. But what has this truth that I recognise to do with my behaviour? Why should I *adopt* that course of action rather than some other? The fact that the course of action is obligatory is presumably meant to be a reason for adopting it; the fact that it would, if adopted, start on a Wednesday presumably is not. But why this difference? Why is some information about the properties of things and of actions irrelevant to questions about what is to be done, while some other information apparently is not? Moral judgments, it seems, like other judgments, convey information: what is it about the information they convey which makes it important for, or even relevant to, our decisions, our choices, our advice, or our recommendations? We find, once again, that intuitionism has nothing to say here: in that theory the relevance of moral judgments to conduct appears as a bare assumption, about which, as indeed about almost everything in the subject, there is nothing to be said.

Intuitionism seems, in retrospect, so strange a phenomenon — a body of writing so acute and at the same time so totally unilluminating — that one may wonder how to explain it, what its genesis was. The idea that there is a vast corpus of moral facts about the world — known, but we cannot say how: related to other features of the world, but we cannot explain in what way: overwhelmingly important for our conduct, but we cannot say why — what does this really astonishing idea reflect? One may be tempted to say: the absence of curiosity. And what the absence of curiosity reflects may be the absence of doubt. One seeks to explain what one feels to be in need of explanation: where everything seems obvious one may feel that there is nothing to be said. Certainly the intuitionist philosophers of the early part of this century do not strike one as men much beset by moral uncertainties; even if, as was surely the case, they were sometimes uncertain on particular questions, they had no *general* uncertainties about the status of morals; what they called 'the facts' of morality were for them simply there, simply given, in the nature of things, standing in need from the theorist of nothing but clear recognition. Their notion that moral judgment was properly to be described on the model of the very simplest assertions of fact was partly attributable, and importantly attributable, to a certain poverty of philosophical apparatus; their general views about 'judgment' seemed to admit no alternative possibility. But it is also important that this theoretical poverty, with the bald simplicity of doctrine which it imposed, was not felt to involve any unacceptable consequences. Why should room be left for uncertainty, if one does not feel any? Why, unless from confusion, should one ask for the obvious to be explained?

III. EMOTIVISM

Ross's *Foundations of Ethics* contains what will perhaps prove to have been the last systematic exposition of pure intuitionist doctrine. When it was published in 1939 there had already begun to emerge the view, or family of views, which was shortly to succeed that doctrine in the centre of the stage. This congeries of views, which is commonly and conveniently labelled 'emotivism', certainly breaks sharply away from the intuitionist point of view; and it was thought for some years, by very many, to have brought great illumination to the study of ethics. It is, perhaps, a desirable thing in itself to change one's point of view from time to time; but it is not really clear that, in any other respect, the new point of view was much of an advance on the old one. It brought some points into prominence that had previously been much neglected; but it imported also some new confusions that had not previously been made.

The first impetus towards emotivism as an ethical theory did not in fact come from moral philosophy itself. It had been, as we have noted, an almost unconscious assumption of the intuitionists that 'moral propositions' asserted a certain kind of fact — that there were certain moral properties actually possessed by certain entities, and that (affirmative) moral judgments simply asserted of those entities that they had those properties. It seems unlikely that this general assumption was made solely for the reason that it seemed particularly well in place in the characterisation of moral judgments; on the contrary, the supposition that moral judgments were of that nature seems to have been made, at times even somewhat uneasily, as a consequence of the quite general supposition that affirmative subject-predicate judgments were *all* of that nature — they ascribed some 'property' or 'character' to that which was designated by the grammatical subject of the judgment. Rather similarly, the view that moral judgments were not of that nature was evidently first arrived at, not because on examination they appeared not in fact to be of that nature, but because it followed from a quite different and quite general philosophical doctrine that they *could* not be of that nature.

The general doctrine in question is the, by now, notorious *Grundgedanke* of the Logical Positivists, that there are just two species of significant propositions — tautologies, and empirically verifiable assertions of fact. Since, naturally and rightly, the Positivists were disinclined to swallow 'intuition' as a respectable means of verification, and since no one was disposed to maintain that moral judgments in general were either tautologous or verifiable by ordinary sense-experience, it followed that they could not be significant propositions: they could not really be, as their grammatical form might lead one to suppose, assertions in which genuine 'properties' were ascribed to things, or indeed genuine assertions of any kind at all. They must be, in their grammatical form, mere masqueraders.

What, then, were they? One rather feels that those who first encountered this problem did not greatly care; nevertheless, they were ready to hazard one or two suggestions. Carnap, for instance, observing that so-called moral judgments were often employed in seeking to direct and influence conduct, threw out the idea that they were really *commands*: 'You ought not to steal' was a misleading way of saying 'Don't steal', 'Kindness is good' of saying 'Be kind'.[8] Schlick, somewhat similarly, suggested that so-called moral judgments really formulated *rules*, and that the only real question for a 'science of ethics' was the psychological question why certain rules come to be adopted.[9] Ayer, in the very succinct sketch which he offers, in *Language, Truth, and Logic* (1936), of an ethical theory, prefers to pick out the point, surely a correct one, that moral judgments often serve to express the feelings of the speaker: it is suggested that this is essentially all that they ever do. Thus in saying, for example, that birth-control is wicked I am not really saying anything, true or false, about birth-control, but merely mentioning it and 'evincing' my disapproval, disgust, or hostility.

19

The objection most warmly urged at the time against this line of thinking was that it threatened to undermine the rationality of morals. One might at first sight be inclined to wonder why this should have been so; for surely it is not the case that, as between commands, or rules, or expressions of feeling, there is never anything to choose on rational grounds? Commands and rules may conflict, very much as propositions may; and some may be reasonable or justified, others may not be. And can I not defend by argument the sentiments I express, or criticise the feelings of another as misplaced or unwarranted? Nevertheless, there was genuine force in the critics' objection. For a command is justified if what it enjoins is the right thing to do: a rule is a good rule if the conduct it requires is desirable conduct: my expression of disgust is warranted if its object is actually disgusting. But such justifying clauses, of course, can function genuinely as giving *reasons* only if they do not themselves express merely further commands, or rules, or personal feelings — whereas, on the line of thinking briefly sketched above, this is *all* that such clauses could ever be construed as doing. It thus appeared that what we ordinarily think of as argument in these contexts is really no more than conflict in another guise; my 'reasons' really do nothing but repeat my original utterance, and showing that I am right is not really distinguishable from carrying my point. It might, of course, effectively have been replied that the intuitionist picture itself leaves no room for the rationality of morals; for, in that picture, moral disagreement reduces to a bare divergence of 'intuitions', to a blank disagreement about which there is nothing to be said. The intuitionist, to be sure, supposes that moral utterances have truth-values; but it is not much use to *say* that my judgment is true and yours is false, if in principle no means are to hand of showing this to be so. But this is only to say that, on this score, both parties were vulnerable.

But we may say that, in any case, the ideas thrown out by Carnap, Schlick, and Ayer were scarcely more than sighting shots, fired off rather hastily as possible preliminaries to a full-blown campaign, by philosophers whose real interests were not in moral philosophy at all. It was always obvious that at least they left a great deal more to be said; but no doubt they did not seriously aspire to completeness. The account offered by C. L. Stevenson in his very influential book *Ethics and Language* (1944), while closely akin to these earlier ventures, is more careful, more comprehensive, and immensely more elaborately presented. There are three main pillars upon which this account stands, and we must first set out what these are.

(ii) C. L. STEVENSON: BELIEFS, ATTITUDES, 'EMOTIVE MEANING'

First, a distinction is sought to be drawn between *beliefs* and *attitudes*. Consider, for instance (to take a non-moral case), a proposal to devalue the pound sterling: and let us suppose that we have two economists whose beliefs concerning this proposal are exactly the same. They are in full agreement as to what it is that is proposed, and also as to what in fact would be the economic, social, and political consequences of adopting the proposal or, alternatively, of rejecting it. It is still possible — one may think it unlikely, but it seems to be possible — that, notwithstanding this full agreement, their *attitudes* towards the proposal should differ; while agreeing exactly as to what the proposal is and would imply, one might be in favour of it, the other against. It would be conceded, no doubt, that most disagreements in attitude rest on, or are due to, disagreements in belief; when one person favours what another opposes, a full enquiry into the situation will usually bring out that they hold somewhat different beliefs as to the nature, or immediate or perhaps very remote effects or consequences, of the matter at issue. It would be conceded also that it might often be exceedingly difficult to show that disagreement in attitude did *not* thus rest on disagreement in belief; for how could one ever be sure that one had established agreement in belief on *all* matters which either party might take to be relevant, however remotely, to the point at issue? Nevertheless, it would be held that the distinction is perfectly clear in theory: disagreement in attitude is plainly *different* from disagreement in belief, hard though it may be to distinguish sharply, in actual cases, between one species of disagreement and the other. We may add that, just as there may be agreement in belief and disagreement in attitude, there may, of course, occur agreement in attitude and disagreement in belief.

Second, there is introduced the notion of 'emotive meaning' — whence the name 'emotivism'. Consider, for instance, the words 'German' and 'Boche'. There is a sense in which these words have exactly the same meaning: they are applicable to exactly the same things, for instance to the members of a certain European nation, and applicable to them, furthermore, on exactly the same basis, or in virtue of just the same facts; there would be no evidential difference between establishing that Fritz was a German and that Fritz was a Boche. Nevertheless, it is plain that the terms do differ in some way. In what way? The difference is, surely, that 'German' is what might be called a neutral expression; it signifies merely membership of a certain nation. 'Boche', on the other hand, is far from neutral. While it too signifies membership of a certain nation, its use also typically expresses the speaker's hostility to or contempt for that nation, and is liable, and often deliberately intended, to evoke similar hostility and contempt on the part of his audience. The two terms, then, are said to have the same 'descriptive meaning'; but 'Boche' has also a certain 'emotive meaning', consisting in the fact that it commonly both expresses, and is liable to arouse, certain feelings towards that to which it is applied. In general, those words are said to have emotive meaning which, besides standardly and neutrally signifying what, if anything, they do signify, also standardly express, and are liable to arouse, favourable or unfavourable feelings or attitudes towards that to which they are applied. (I say 'if anything' since, it is suggested, there are words — 'Hurrah!' for example — which have little or no descriptive meaning at all, but are *purely* emotive.) It may be added that, while any term's emotive meaning will normally be somewhat dependent on or connected with its descriptive meaning, it is quite possible that, if the normal attitudes or feelings of its users change, while its descriptive meaning remains more or less constant, its emotive meaning may dwindle or vanish, or may even be reversed. It is not very long, for instance, since the word 'democracy' commonly expressed and aroused feelings of alarm and despondency — though, indeed, it is also not entirely clear in this case either that the term has any very definite descriptive meaning, or that its descriptive meaning may not gradually have shifted as well.

Third, after these preliminaries the thesis is advanced that it is the distinctive feature of moral judgment not to convey the speaker's *beliefs*, but to evince his *attitudes*; and not to add to or alter the *beliefs* of the person addressed, but to influence his *attitudes* and hence, in all probability, his conduct. Moral discourse (in a nutshell) is primarily not informative but *influential*; it may modify beliefs incidentally, but attitudes primarily.[10] It was this point, it would be said, that the intuitionists had dimly in view when they insisted that moral predicates were not reducible to other, i.e. to purely descriptive, predicates. They were aware that in some way a moral judgment upon, say, a proposed course of action was not only not equivalent to, but was quite unlike, any mere description of the course of action proposed. They quite failed to see, however, just what the point was here. Because of their addiction to the assumed adjective–property equation, they were led to represent moral judgment merely as a peculiar kind of description, consisting in the ascription to things of peculiar, 'non-natural', *sui generis* properties. But this fudged the very point that they had dimly in view. For a queer sort of information is still, after all, information; description in terms of strange *sui generis* properties is still description. They thus failed to bring out the distinction between beliefs and attitudes, reducing attitudes in fact to a mysterious species of beliefs; and thus, still representing moral judgments as purely informative, they could make no sense at all of the essential connection between moral discourse and our attitudes, decisions, choices, and in general, behaviour. Most moral predicates, no doubt, do stand for properties. When we are told for example, that some person is generous or honest, we learn something, quite descriptively, of what sort of person he is and what he tends to do. But it is not this, the emotivist insists, that makes the judgment about him a moral one; what makes it moral is that the terms applied to him also both express and induce a *favourable attitude* towards him, both evince and arouse certain feelings towards that person. And this is not the ascription to him of an extra property; it is quite unlike the ascription of properties; it is, rather, 'emotive', 'dynamic', a question of influence.

It will be clear from this brief and somewhat simplified sketch of emotivism that this doctrine has certain undeniable and important merits. It completely does away with the perplexing intuitionist mythology of 'non-natural' *sui generis* moral properties, and indeed with 'intuition' itself. 'Emotive meaning', by contrast, points to a real phenomenon of considerable theoretical interest and practical importance. Moreover, while, as we have just mentioned, intuitionism offers no intelligible account of the relation between moral judgment and conduct, the emotivist thesis connects moral judgment with conduct in a perfectly intelligible and (within limits) clear and definite manner. Unfortunately, as we must now observe, this connection, while possessing the merit of being intelligible, clear, and definite, has the demerit also of being completely wrong, and indeed, in a certain sense, disastrously wrong.

(iii) THE ERRORS OF EMOTIVISM

It is the central thesis of emotivism that moral discourse is essentially to be characterised by reference to its purpose: as Stevenson puts it, the 'major use' of ethical judgments is 'not to indicate facts, but to *create an influence*'.[11] In any moral discourse the characteristic purpose of the speaker is to influence, not the beliefs, but the *attitudes* of his audience.

One point, I take it, will be immediately obvious — namely, that this purpose is in no way distinctive of moral discourse. It may well be the case, as Stevenson says, that ethical statements are 'social instruments' for the control, redirection, and modification of 'attitudes'; but so also are advertising posters, television commercials, political speeches, threats, 'committed' works of literature, bribes, and so on. Suppose, for example, that I wish to 'create an influence' in favour of larger families in England. It is clear that there are *many* ways in which I might try to do this — many species of 'social instruments' of which I might avail myself for the purpose in hand. I might, indeed, engage in moral exhortation, assuring the populace that they ought, that it is right, that perhaps it is positively their duty, to engage more copiously in procreation. But alternatively, or in addition, I might buy space on bill-boards or time on television, spreading abroad the image of happy, smiling parents among troops of genial, healthy infants. I might make childless adults liable to national service, and give large tax reliefs to the philoprogenitive. I might seek to make out that large families are a mark of the aristocracy, or write novels about the miseries of neglected and solitary old age. It is obvious that all these are ways of 'creating an influence', that they all have the purpose of modifying 'attitudes' and, in consequence, conduct: so that, even if it is true that moral discourse has this purpose, moral discourse is not thereby distinguished from many other things.

But now, is it true that moral discourse *has* this purpose? It is not difficult to see that the answer is: not necessarily, not always. If I set out to 'create an influence' by issuing a moral utterance, then presumably (i) I suppose that my audience does not already have the 'attitude' which my utterance is calculated to promote; also (ii) I wish my audience to have this attitude; and (iii) I think it at least possible that my issuing the utterance will tend to promote adoption of this attitude. But then I may, of course, quite well issue a moral utterance when any or all of these conditions fail. I may be conversing with someone whose 'attitude' I know to be the same as mine, whom, so to speak, I cannot *move* because he is there already. I may be concerned merely to make my own 'attitude' known to some person to whose reactions to it I am entirely indifferent or, again, who to my knowledge does not care a straw for my opinion. Moral discourse is not always so 'dynamic' as all that. A good deal of what might be called moral chat goes on in the comfortable belief that all parties to it are firmly, perhaps smugly, at one in the attitudes exposed; and though the expression of moral judgments to persons one does not care, or is not able, to influence may be thought somewhat pointless, it is not impossible, and may have some other than the usual point. Thus the alleged dynamic purpose of moral discourse is not only not distinctive of it; it may be quite absent and the discourse be not the less moral for that.

But emotivism is perhaps most seriously in error in its account of the way in which, in moral discourse, 'influence' is exerted. The aptness of moral language to the supposed dynamic ends of moral discourse is sought to be explained by reference to 'emotive meaning'. It is, it is said, because moral words have emotive (and not merely descriptive) meanings that they can play the double role of *evincing* the attitude of the speaker, and exerting *influence* upon the attitude of the addressee. They express my feelings, and will tend to arouse yours. But it is not, I think, difficult to see that this is all wrong, and importantly so.

What *are* emotive words? Why is it that a speaker or writer may be blamed, or in other cases praised, for his employment of emotive language? Emotive words are words that appeal to the feelings or (as of course the term itself suggests) to the emotions. Now this is sometimes, as for instance in certain kinds of literary work, a good thing; for here it may be the intended and entirely proper purpose to appeal to, to stir, the feelings of a reader or an audience. But of course it may often be highly undesirable. A Treasury official, for instance, summarising or commenting upon some issue of economic policy, would justly be rebuked if his minute or memorandum were couched in highly emotive terms. He will do well to avoid, even if he is tempted by, such epithets as 'scandalous', 'fatuous', 'nauseating', or 'bird-brained'. For such language is inimical to the calm and balance of bureaucratic judgment; whereas it is such as his Minister, for example, might use with propriety and effect in the very different context of his electioneering. Now it is clear enough that some moral terms are, in this sense, somewhat emotive; the feelings are quite liable to stir at such a term as 'heroic', and to stir in an opposite sense at such a term as 'blackguardly' or 'vicious'. But the pulses do not beat faster at encountering the word 'right'; there is nothing particularly stirring about 'good', or 'ought';

and if the Treasury official writes, for instance, that the financier's proposition is entirely honest, and even generous, he could scarcely be criticised for using emotive language. The fact is that expressing and appealing to the feelings is incidental to, and actually quite rare in, moral discourse, much as exerting influence is incidental to, and often quite absent from, making moral judgments. 'It would be monstrous to do that!' expresses my feelings, and may stimulate yours; but 'It would be wrong to do that' is most unlikely to do either. It expresses an opinion, not a state of emotional excitement; it gives you, perhaps, my advice against doing something, not a stimulus towards emotional revulsion from doing it. There is nothing, in short, necessarily *emotive* about moral criticism or approval; moral advice may be given in entirely dispassionate terms. Equally, of course, a piece of discourse may be highly emotive but unconcerned with morals; and one's feelings may quite well run counter to one's moral views.

It is not difficult, in the light of these criticisms, to appreciate why to many the implications of emotivism seemed peculiarly objectionable. We see that it was the characteristic feature — it was put forward, indeed, as the chief claim to originality — of emotivist doctrine to turn away from the informative content, if any, of moral discourse, and instead to locate the essence of moral discourse in its *effects*. In place of the orthodox intuitionist view that a moral judgment, like other judgments, *stated* something and was typically intended to inform, the view was advanced that a moral judgment essentially *did* something, and was typically intended to produce a certain effect. But much as the intuitionists were prevented, by their apparatus of direct 'intuition' and 'self-evident' facts, from having anything of interest to say about moral argument, so, or even more so, for quite different reasons were the emotivists. Briefly: if it is held that a certain kind of discourse is employed essentially to produce an effect, it must follow that the criterion by which such discourse is to be appraised must essentially be the criterion simply of effectiveness. If the point of some tract of discourse is, say, essentially to influence your attitude, to arouse your feelings, then that tract of discourse is good if it succeeds, or is well calculated to succeed, in doing this; it is bad, vulnerable to criticism, if it proves inefficacious, or might have been expected to do so. In logic, it is possible to make a quite clear distinction between an argument's being valid, and an argument's producing conviction; we can well say that a proof, though it convinced, contained a fallacy, or that it was a valid proof, though it happened that no one was convinced by it. The emotivist view leaves no room for an analogous distinction in ethics. Questions of belief, it is allowed, may be rationally debated; we may distinguish here between truth and falsehood, good evidence or bad, between mere prejudice and well-founded belief, belief for good reasons. But on the characteristically moral (as it was supposed) matter of attitudes, there could be no such distinctions; a moral 'argument' so-called might produce its effect or fail to do so, but there was no room for consideration, as a *further question*, as to whether it was a good argument or a bad one. In this way moral discourse emerged — notwithstanding much strenuous special pleading — as essentially in the same boat with propaganda, or advertising, or even intimidation; it was intended to influence people, to affect their feelings and behaviour, and was to be assessed not as rational, in terms of good reasons or bad reasons, but as effective or ineffective, in terms of what did or did not yield the results intended. There were many who were able to swallow this startling conclusion; but it was felt in many quarters that something must have gone very wrong.

What *had* gone wrong? Chiefly, I think, two things. First, the emotivists were understandably over-impressed by their idea of bringing in the *purpose*, or function, of moral discourse. It is true that the intuitionists had been distressingly silent on this point. Their view of moral judgments as straightforward (though in certain respects peculiar) truths and falsehoods had appeared to make a mystery of the relation of such judgments to conduct; they seemed not to have considered at all what moral discourse is *for*. But the emotivists, one might say, were inclined merely to go to the opposite extreme — to dwell, that is, so exclusively on what moral discourse is for, that they scarcely raised seriously the question what it actually is. It is a good thing, no doubt, to appreciate *that* moral discourse is quite often directed to influencing 'attitudes'; but it should have been considered more carefully *how* it does so. For the general purpose, as we have seen, is not an invariable feature of moral utterances and, more importantly, does not distinguish such utterances from many other kinds of linguistic — and for that matter non-linguistic — proceedings.

Second, so far as emotivists did consider how it is that moral discourse may influence attitudes, their account was inadequate, or indeed seriously mistaken. The trouble here arose, in large part, from a certain crudity in their notion of what 'attitudes' are. There was a constant tendency to identify attitudes with *feelings* — to identify, say, my disapproval of someone's behaviour with the disgust or revulsion which I may feel on witnessing it. But this was not merely wrong: it was disastrously wrong. For as a consequence, expressing my disapproval of someone's behaviour became identified with the widely different phenomenon of 'giving vent' to my feelings about it; and my seeking to change someone else's 'attitude' came to be represented as simply an attempt to work on his emotions. Hence the blunder of supposing that moral words as such have 'emotive meaning'; for if I am 'venting' my feelings and working on yours, must it not be the case that I am using emotive language? Thence, finally, the conclusion that moral discourse is essentially non-rational, a matter not of argument but of psychological pressure, not of reasons but of efficacious manipulation. Intuitionism had left gaps — indeed, scarcely anything except gaps — in moral philosophy; but there was a great quantity of muddle in the filling which emotivism supplied.

IV. PRESCRIPTIVISM

(i) ADVICE VERSUS INFLUENCE

The next turn taken by moral philosophy in this century can best be introduced as — and was, I think it is true to say, in fact introduced as — an amendment to emotivism. The amendment in question, which is principally the work of R. M. Hare, has been extremely influential, and in certain respects is genuinely illuminating. I believe it to be by no means free from confusion; but its virtues and deficiencies, we may hope, will prove alike instructive.

Let us look back once again to the implicit assumption of intuitionism that moral discourse is essentially informative — that a moral judgment typically states, or otherwise alludes to, the ethical fact that some moral property is possessed by some subject. It was, as we have seen, the central tenet of emotivism that this implicit assumption is false — that, even if a moral judgment does inform, or state some fact, this is not the essence of the case. With this tenet of emotivism Hare emphatically agrees. He too insists that the purveying of information, even if the information be supposed to be of a peculiar 'non-natural' kind, is not the essence of moral discourse, but is at most purely incidental to it. But whereas, in rejecting the intuitionists' implicit assumption, the emotivists had concluded that the essence of moral discourse lay in its use to 'create an influence', to *affect* people's feelings ('attitudes') and so their behaviour, Hare contends that the essence is not influence but *guidance*.[12] In saying to you, for example, 'You ought to repay the money' I am not, indeed, merely stating some fact; but nor am I, primarily or necessarily, seeking to get you to do something; I am, essentially, telling you *what to do*. You have, as it were — so Hare puts it — raised the question 'What shall I do?'; and I have answered that question. Actually getting, moving, or inducing you to do what

I tell you to do is something else again. Influencing your behaviour may possibly be an effect, and is quite likely indeed, to be the intended effect, of the answer I give you, of my issuing that moral utterance; but it is still essential to distinguish my telling you what to do from any effects or consequences, actual or intended, of my so telling you — what I am doing *in* saying 'You ought to repay the money', from what I may (possibly) hope to achieve *by* saying it.[13]

At least one great virtue of this amendment will be plain enough; it seems at once to enable us to escape the conclusion that moral discourse is fundamentally non-rational. The problem of getting somebody to do something, or of influencing his feelings with that end in view, is simply the problem of employing *effective* means to that end; even if in some case I should decide that talking to a person — as an alternative, say, to frightening him, or feeding him drugs — will influence him most effectively, it may well not matter whether or not he understands what I say, or whether or not what I say makes any sense. A dictum, to be 'emotively' effective, need not necessarily be understood, or even be intelligible; it will be right — for the purpose — on the sole condition that it works. But about guidance, clearly, quite other questions can be raised. It is essential, here, that you should understand what I tell you; you may ask me for my reasons, and consider whether the reasons I give you are good or bad; my answer to your question may be the right answer even if you do not accept it, or wrong even though you accept it without hesitation. To ask for and to give answers to practical questions is plainly and essentially a business for rational beings, and one that can be appraised on rational grounds. We may note the absurdity of the emotivist's notion that one who asks 'What ought I to do?' is 'asking for influence',[14] and by contrast the perfect naturalness of Hare's amendment: he is asking for guidance.

Moral discourse then, Hare holds, is not primarily — though sometimes it may be incidentally — informative; but nor is it essentially — though sometimes it may be incidentally — 'emotive'. It does not serve essentially, though it may do consequentially, to *influence* people, to get them to do things or refrain from doing them; it is, rather, action-guiding, or, in Hare's term 'prescriptive'. Let us consider a little further what this means.

(ii) MORAL DISCOURSE AS 'PRESCRIPTIVE'

Prescriptive discourse, I think we may say quite generally (expounding Hare), is that species of discourse in which practical questions are answered — much as, one might say, informative discourse is that species of discourse which answers requests for information. If you put to me the information-seeking question 'Where do you live?', my answer ('I live in Oxford') is a specimen of informative discourse; if you put to me the practical question 'What ought I to do?', my answer will be a specimen of prescriptive discourse.

Now the simplest of all forms of prescriptive discourse, and also in a sense the basic form, is, in Hare's view, the plain imperative. The palmary case of telling someone what to do is to issue, for instance, the simple imperative 'Go away' — an utterance which may or may not have the effect of *making* its addressee go away, but at any rate *tells* him to. But in Hare's view we cannot properly say, as Carnap once did, that moral judgments just *are* grammatically disguised imperatives, for, as we shall see, moral judgments have certain essential features which simple imperatives may lack. But moral judgments, he holds, do have in common with imperatives the crucial feature that they are 'prescriptive'; and this in fact means, in Hare's view, that a moral judgment — or at any rate a genuine, typical, non-deviant moral judgment — *entails* an imperative. Just as, if a proposition p entails another proposition q, I cannot (consistently) assert or accept p and deny or reject q, so, in Hare's view, I cannot (consistently) assert or accept the moral judgment, say, 'You ought to repay the money' and deny or reject the imperative 'Repay the money'. Now to 'deny' or 'reject' an imperative, Hare holds, is simply, having received it, *not* to act on it, not to do what it says. Thus, the thesis that moral judgments are prescriptive implies that one who accepts the moral judgment that he ought to do X is logically committed to doing X; conversely, that one who does not do X is logically debarred from accepting or affirming the judgment that he ought to do X. My moral judgment that you ought to do X 'guides' your action, not in the sense that it necessarily *moves* you to do X, but in that your accepting my judgment *commits* you to doing X, and your not doing X implies your rejection of my judgment. For in saying that you ought to do it I am implicitly telling you to do it; and if you do not, you have not accepted what I said.

Moral judgments, then, are supposed to resemble imperatives in being 'prescriptive', and to be so, indeed, in virtue of an intimate logical relation to imperatives. But they have, Hare holds, a further most important feature which distinguishes them from at any rate many imperatives. I may, on a whim of the moment, tell you in particular to go away on this particular occasion, without thereby being logically committed to saying or doing anything in particular on any other occasion; the singular imperative 'Go away', issued to you here and now, does not *bind* me to taking any particular line elsewhere or elsewhen. If on another occasion, perhaps another exactly similar occasion, I happen to want you not to go away, I may issue the imperative 'Don't go' without logical impropriety. Not so, however, with moral judgments. For the moral judgment that I make in a certain situation must be founded on, made in virtue of, certain features *of* that situation; and accordingly I must, in consistency, be prepared to make the same judgment in any situation which shares those features (and does not differ in any other relevant respect). Such a judgment as 'You ought to repay the money' is, in Hare's term, universalisable; that is, if I commit myself to this judgment in your particular case, I thereby commit myself to the view that anybody — including, most importantly, myself — in the circumstances in which you now are ought to act in that way. I cannot, without logical impropriety, issue a different judgment in another case, unless I can show that other case to be different in some relevant respect. Or if I judge differently some other case which I cannot show to be relevantly different, then I am bound to correct or withdraw my original judgment. Moral judgments, in effect, cannot be, as imperatives may be, purely and completely singular; in judging this case, we implicitly judge any case of this *kind*, and cannot accordingly judge differently other cases of the *same* kind.

We have before us, then, the thesis 'that moral judgments are a kind of *prescriptive* judgments, and that they are distinguished from other judgments of this class by being *universalisable*.'[15] I shall now argue, first, that moral judgments are *not* essentially prescriptive, and second, that, if that is so, we need not claim for 'universalisability' the importance which Hare, as I think mistakenly, claims for it.

(iii) TWO VERSIONS OF 'PRESCRIPTIVISM'

I believe that there can be discerned, encapsulated in what we may call the prescriptivist thesis, at least two distinguishable doctrines which call for separate discussion. I begin with the one that seems the more obviously false.

The prescriptivist thesis is, of course, put forward as a quite general thesis about moral discourse — not only, we may note, about moral utterances in general, but even about moral words in general, which are said by Hare to have 'prescriptive meaning'. Now one way in which this thesis might be taken, and in which it has sometimes been put forward, would be this: it is the thesis that there is a certain class of words, which includes that class of words which occur characteristically in moral discourse, whose meaning is to be explained (at least in part) in terms of the performance of a particular 'speech-act', namely, prescribing. That is to say: in any discourse in which those words occur in their standard meanings, it must be the case that the speaker of that discourse is therein prescribing. He is, at any rate in part or implicitly, 'telling someone what to do'.

One might think that, as a general thesis about the occurrence in discourse of moral words, this is too obviously false ever to have been seriously believed. How could it possibly have been supposed that moral discourse, in all its almost endless diversity of forms and contexts, must consist essentially and always in the performance of any *single* speech-act? No one would think of saying this about discourse in general: but moral discourse, discourse in which moral words occur, is not much, if at all, less versatile in this respect than discourse in general; there are at any rate dozens of things which those who employ moral words may therein be doing. They may be prescribing, certainly; but also they may be advising, exhorting, imploring; commanding, condemning, deploring; resolving, confessing, undertaking; and so on, and so on. But here we may note as a possible explanatory factor the fairly obvious fact that, when Hare thinks of 'moral discourse', he thinks first of such discourse as occurring in one particular context — that, namely, in which one speaker addresses to another a moral judgment upon some course of action currently open to, and possibly to be undertaken by, that other person; in which A asks 'What shall I do?', and B answers his question. This half-conscious restriction of context was in fact already present, we may note further, in emotivism; for the context in which one typically 'creates an influence' is that in which one talks to another party with an eye to his present or future behaviour. That Hare is apt to carry over this tacit restriction is evident from his recurrent concern with imperatives,[16] which, of course, are also typically issued by one speaker to another with an eye to what that other is currently to do. Now it is certainly not grossly false to say of imperatives (though it is not quite true either) that they are tied, so to speak, to the performance of a particular speech-act. It is not very badly wrong to say, that is, that one who engages in 'imperative discourse' is therein, in virtue of what imperatives are, performing the speech-act of telling someone what to do. But if, as Hare seems to, one half-consciously restricts one's attention to the kinds of contexts in which imperatives would naturally occur, then it may seem fairly plausible to say that 'moral judgment' too consists in the performance of, is tied to, one particular speech-act, that of prescribing. This is not, indeed, a truth about moral judgment, still less about moral *words*; it might be a truth, at best, about the particular class of moral utterances which might naturally be issued in that particular kind of situation. But if the very narrow restriction of context is not noticed, the gross absurdity of the generalised thesis may not be noticed either.

The prescriptivist thesis, however, cannot yet be dismissed; for it is not merely the gross absurdity that we have just considered. Though that plainly false doctrine has certainly been propounded in its name — and even, at the price of desperate paradox, explicitly defended —the thesis is susceptible of a much less absurd interpretation. The false doctrine, in fact, has probably managed to hold the field not only because the above-mentioned half-conscious restrictions have masked its full absurdity, but also because it has not been properly distinguished from the more plausible doctrine that we have now to consider.

The more plausible doctrine, and the one that is really central in Hare's account, is that moral discourse is prescriptive in the sense that, in discourse of this kind, there obtains a quite special connection between words and deeds. Here we may glance once again at the comparison with imperatives. Suppose that I issue to you the imperative utterance 'Spare that tree'; in what would acceptance by you of my utterance consist? It seems that we must say: it would consist in your *doing* what I say, namely, sparing that tree. Generalising, we may say that imperative discourse is such that acceptance of what is said in that mode consists in appropriate *action* on the part of those to whom it is addressed: you have not accepted what I said if you do not do as I say. Now it is in this respect, Hare believes, that moral discourse is analogous, that it too is prescriptive. We need not embrace (though he sometimes does) the rather obvious falsehood that to issue a moral utterance is always to tell someone what to do; but we can and must say that any proposition in morals, whatever the speaker may be doing in issuing that proposition, is such that acceptance of it consists in acting in a certain way, either here and now, or if the appropriate circumstances should arise. Moreover (since moral judgments, unlike imperatives, are universalisable and 'apply' to the speaker himself no less than to other persons), any proposition in morals also commits the speaker to acting in a certain way; if he does not so act, then he does not mean what he says. If I remark to you that it was very wrong of Jenkins to get so horribly drunk at his daughter's wedding, I surely am not telling you — still less myself — not to get horribly drunk at weddings of daughters: perhaps we have no daughters, or our daughters are already firmly settled in the married state, and in any case I am talking about Jenkins, not you or me. Nevertheless, my remark is such that anyone who really accepts it stays sober at his daughter's wedding and on occasions of that *kind*, or at least, like you and me, would do so if so placed. If you would not, then you do not really accept what I say: and if I would not, then I do not sincerely mean what I say. It is not only that, as we are told, actions speak louder than words; it is that, in the case of prescriptive discourse, actions confirm or refute words, in acting we 'accept' or 'reject' them. And it is, of course, by no means obviously false that moral discourse is prescriptive in this sense; for we should all be inclined to agree that, as Hare puts it, 'If we were to ask of a person "What are his moral principles?" the way in which we could be most sure of a true answer would be by studying what he *did*'.[17]

Now that there is, in moral discourse, this kind of close connection, of interdependence, between words and deeds is, at the very least, a very plausible view. It needs, I think, to be hedged and qualified in certain respects, some of great importance; but let us for the moment postpone those operations. We must first consider whether, assuming this view to be correct, it follows that in *this* sense the prescriptivist thesis is true.

This may seem at first sight to be a very extraordinary question; for it may seem that Hare's prescriptivist doctrine — not indeed in its absurd, but in its other, more persuasive sense — just *is* the doctrine that in moral discourse this interdependence of words and deeds obtains. But this is not so. Prescriptivism has, I think, looked persuasive to many because it has been thought simply to be this doctrine. But it is not; for it not only asserts this interdependence, it seeks to explain it; and the explanation is far indeed from being obviously correct.

We come up here, once again, against the seductive influence of the imperative model. It is indeed true (or true enough) to say that to accept the imperative 'Spare that tree' just is to spare that tree, and that accordingly we have a case here of a very intimate relation between words and deeds. The relation in this case, furthermore, is susceptible of relatively simple explanation. The deed — or non-deed perhaps — of sparing that tree is thus intimately related to the words in question in that the words *prescribe* that course of action; and it is for that reason that the course of action constitutes acceptance of what was said, and any other course of action would constitute its rejection. Now the prescriptivist thesis says (as its name implies) not only plausibly, that in moral discourse there obtains a comparably intimate relation between words and deeds, but also, much less plausibly, that that relation holds here for the *same reason*: the words prescribe, and the deeds are consonant or dissonant with the words in so far as, and because, they do or do not follow the prescription given. It is not exactly that (as on the absurd view) to issue a moral judgment is itself always actually to prescribe; it is rather that any moral judgment either is, or presupposes, or implies, or both, a prescription. As we put it at an earlier stage, it 'entails an imperative'; and it is in virtue of *that* that our relation obtains here between words and deeds, and that moral discourse can be said in general to be 'action-guiding'.

But why, we may now ask, should the relation be explained in this way? Some may have thought — some have certainly written as if they thought — that it must be explained in this way because there is no other way; the *only* way in which deeds can be consonant, or dissonant, with words is for their doing to be, or not be, what the words *prescribe*. But it is really quite obvious that this is not the only possibility; there are dozens of others. I may express a liking for the modern dance, and my behaviour may show that I do not really like it at all. I may say that I want a classless society, and my actions may betray that I really want no such thing. I may express a resolution always to be kind to children, and so act as to show that I was wholly insincere in doing so. I may say that my ideal is perfect self-mortification, and live in a way that makes clear that this is idle verbiage. I may say that I value social justice above all things, and show in practice, when it comes to the crunch, that I value many things much more.

And so on and so on. Thus, from the fact, if it be a fact, that a man's moral principles are revealed most decisively in his behaviour, it does not follow in the least that those principles have to be conceived as, or as implying, *prescriptions*. They might, so far as that point goes, equally well be conceived as expressions of taste or of approval, as avowals of wants or aims, as views about values or ideals, as resolutions, as beliefs about interests, and in many other ways too. On this score at any rate, 'Eating people is wrong' is no more closely akin to 'Don't eat people' than it is to 'I don't want people to be eaten': for in each of these cases the eating of people, or looking on complacently while people are eaten, would be in some sort of conflict with, even in a sense would contradict, what is said. Why then should we, having conceded, as we must, that moral judgments in general *are* not imperatives, still maintain that they are all in this respect *like* imperatives, that their relation to conduct is to be explained in the same way?

(iv) MORAL DISCOURSE AND CONDUCT

The fact is, as I think we are now in a position to see, that the thesis of 'prescriptivism' errs, at bottom, in attempting to answer an impossible question — a question, that is, to which *any* answer would be bound to be wrong. Imperative discourse, as we may say reasonably enough, is in some way intimately related to conduct; and here we may go on to ask: in what way, exactly? Now this is a question, as it happens, that has quite a good answer; for in virtue of what imperatives are, it is broadly true to say that one who issues an imperative, employs an imperative expression, is therein telling someone to do something, whose behaviour may accordingly conform with, or go against, what is said. Now Hare, it appears, goes on from this point to ask the same question of *moral* discourse — this is intimately related to conduct: in what way, exactly? But here we have a question without an answer; for, whereas imperative expressions form a particular grammatical class whose members (roughly) are standardly employed for one particular purpose in one particular type of situation, 'moral expressions' are of the utmost grammatical diversity, may occur in very widely varied types of situations, and may be employed in doing very many quite different things. Thus, while it is reasonable to suppose that the relation of imperatives to conduct can be characterised, broadly at any rate, in *one* way, it is entirely unreasonable to suppose that the same can be done for 'moral discourse'. Sometimes, certainly — namely, in that type of situation which seems always to be at the front of Hare's mind — moral discourse will be prescriptive: the speaker will be, roughly speaking, telling another person what to do, instructing, advising, or 'guiding' him. But at other times not. As Nowell-Smith very properly remarks: 'The words with which moral philosophers have especially to do . . . play many different parts. They are used to express tastes and preferences, to express decisions and choices, to criticise, grade, and evaluate, to advise, admonish, warn, persuade and dissuade, to praise, encourage and reprove, to promulgate and draw attention to rules; and doubtless for other purposes also.'[18] It is probably true that in all these cases *someone's* conduct will be *somehow* related to, consonant or dissonant with, what the speaker says — sometimes his own conduct, sometimes that of the person he addresses, sometimes that of specific other persons, or of people in general. But the actual relations, quite clearly, will be widely diverse, and not to be summed up in any *single* formula whatever.

At the end of the last section we took note of a number of different ways in which deeds, as we put it, may be 'consonant or dissonant' with words, otherwise than by being or not being what the words prescribe. We can now see that it would be a complete mistake to raise the question which of these ways is exemplified, or even most nearly exemplified, in moral discourse. For the fact is that they all are; and so are a great many more. Resolutions on my own part, advice offered to another; the profession of aspirations or ideals; the expression of distaste, criticism, or commendation; reference to wants of my own, or to the needs or aims or interests of others — *all* of these commonly occur in 'moral discourse', just as they occur also, of course, in discourse that is not moral. In each case there is, no doubt, some relation to conduct, but by no means the same kind of relation in every case. We thus find in the end that our two versions of prescriptivism err, not indeed in quite the same way, but still in very similar ways. In its absurd form the doctrine seeks to incorporate into 'moral discourse', and even into the meanings of moral words, the performance of just one particular speech-act, that of *prescribing* — as if, whatever the moral discourser is saying and in whatever situation, this is the *only* thing that he can ever be doing. The other version is not so blatantly misguided as this, for it does not construe the term 'prescriptive' so narrowly as to imply that one who uses a prescriptive expression must always be, literally and strictly, prescribing; the suggestion is only that what is thus said is always related very intimately to what is done. But at this point there creeps in the very similar error of supposing that this relation is always to be explained in the same way, and explained, furthermore, on the model of actual prescription. But that moral discourse in general is related to conduct in *one* way is no more true than that one who engages in moral discourse is always doing *one* thing.

A legislator, a judge, an advocate, and a juryman may all engage in 'legal discourse'. But on the one hand they will not, of course, all therein be doing the same one thing; nor, obviously, will the things they are severally saying be related in any one way, though probably all are in some way, to human conduct. A possible 'prescriptive theory of legal discourse' — which would consist, perhaps, in taking the language of *legislation* as that in terms of which all legal talk would be sought to be explained — would share most of the merits and demerits of its analogue in ethics. It would throw practically no light on the law. I am not suggesting, of course, that there is no truth whatever in 'prescriptivism' as an ethical theory; but I do suggest that there is less truth than falsehood. The grain of truth is to be located in the very general claim that 'moral discourse' is not purely, theoretically, informative — it bears on conduct, what is done may be in conflict or in harmony with what is said. But in so far as the theory does not merely state this unexceptionable platitude, but purports to offer an explanation of it, it appears to me to be completely mistaken — and mistaken, not only in that it wrongly proposes 'prescribing' as the link between moral words and deeds, but, more seriously, in that it tacitly embodies the grossly false idea that there is some *one* way in which this linkage can usefully be described. The question how 'moral discourse' bears on conduct really needs to be separately considered for many quite different kinds of moral utterance, and for many quite different situations or contexts in which moral utterances may occur. It seems a considerable disservice to obscure this diversity beneath the appearance of a single, rather simple, monolithic doctrine.

We are left, then, with a number of questions still disconcertingly open. The intuitionist's characterisation of moral discourse we have seen to be distressingly taciturn. That moral discourse is 'emotive' is, we have further observed, not universally true nor in any case distinctive. But we now have to say, it appears, much the same about prescriptivism. For if moral discourse is in some contexts prescriptive, that is not because it is moral discourse, but because it is, in those particular contexts, discourse in which prescribing happens to be going on. How then *is* moral discourse to be, in general, distinguished? What makes it moral? What, in fact, does 'moral' mean? This is a question, far too seldom considered with the care and attention it deserves, to which we shall revert, somewhat sketchily, in later sections.

(v) ARGUMENT IN MORALS

We took note, in introducing the prescriptivist amendment to emotivism, that it had at least *prima facie* the considerable advantage of not representing moral discourse and debate as fundamentally non-rational. To guide, we observed, unlike to influence, is essentially to engage in a rational activity; advice, whether accepted or not, may be good or bad, I may have good or bad reasons for offering you the guidance I do. But now we must observe that this advantage turns out to be illusory: prescriptivism too cannot find much place for argument.

In Hare's own account of moral reasoning, very great importance is attached to the feature of moral judgment, already mentioned, which he calls 'universalisability'. It is, Hare seems to say — and, as we shall see, not without reason — solely in virtue of this feature that argument, properly so called, is possible in morals; and he is naturally disposed to make quite substantial claims as to what such argument can achieve. Now to say that any proposition in morals is 'universalisable' is, as we briefly noted earlier, to say that one who affirms or accepts that proposition is thereby committed — as a matter of logic — to a certain view of any cases of a certain kind. For me to assert that you ought not to do X in situation Y commits me, as a matter of logic, to the general 'principle' that no one should do things *like* X in situations *like* Y — 'like' meaning here 'not relevantly distinguishable from'. Generality of this sort is implicit in all moral judgment.

Now one might think at first sight that, while argument on the basis of this feature is certainly possible, yet such argument could not really achieve very much. For what, on the basis of this feature, can be argued about? What is put in issue? It is plain, I think, that what is put in issue is simply consistency. To appeal, in discussion of some moral judgment that I make, to the feature of universalisability is not to raise the question whether my judgment of the case before me is *right*, but only the question whether it is the same as, or compatible with, the judgments that I make or would make of other cases of the same kind. It is not, indeed, that this matter is unimportant. For people are indeed very commonly prone, from prejudice or bigotry or thoughtlessness, to judge differently cases which are not relevantly different — to make, for example, unjustifiable exceptions in favour of themselves or their friends, and to the detriment of foreigners, or political opponents, persons they dislike, or persons whose existence is inconvenient to them. And in such cases they may indeed be logically obliged — though not necessarily induced — to change or amend their judgments, when the requirement of consistent universalisability is forced upon their attention. Nevertheless, if it appears to you that my judgment of some particular case is morally quite wrong, you may well achieve nothing by appealing to universalisability; for all that may emerge may be that I am perfectly prepared to make the same (in your view) wrong judgment of any case of this kind. All my standards and principles may seem to you highly objectionable; but, provided that I apply them consistently in every case, they will be quite invulnerable to any argument of this pattern.

But is this point, one may wonder, too abstractly stated?[19] Is the case we envisage really, and not merely theoretically, a possible one? It is easy to say that, in theory, practically any moral judgment, however objectionable, might be consistently 'universalised', and so might stand unscathed against argument founded upon this consideration. But may it not be the case in fact that not many highly objectionable judgments actually would emerge from such scrutiny unscathed? One might think that this would probably be so for the following reason. What is really objectionable, one might think, about many objectionable moral judgments is that one who makes them does so in disregard of, or without giving proper weight to, the wants, or the needs, or the interests, of those concerned (other than himself); he ignores, let us say, or does not properly consider, the fact that the interests of other persons will be gravely damaged by the course of action which he professes morally to approve. But if so — if he is prepared seriously to hold, as a general principle, that such action to the detriment of others' interests is to be morally approved — we can point out that, in virtue of the condition of universalisability, he is committed to approving of the neglect or damage of *his own* interests if and when, as may occur, he is himself in the position of those whose interests will be damaged by the action in this case. If their interests may properly be neglected now, so, when he finds himself in their shoes, may his. But surely only the most irrational of men could want the neglect or frustration of his own interests; and if so, the requirement of universalisability may seem to impose upon any rational man the condition that, in his practical judgments, he *must* pay that regard to the interests of others which, in general, he would want to be paid to his own interests. And it is plain that this would constitute, in practice, a condition of very substantial moral significance and effect.

I think, however, that there is an important equivocation here. It is true — perhaps even necessarily true — that no rational man *wants* the frustration of what he sees as his own interests, or *likes* it when his interests are frustrated. But then what a man wants, or would like, is scarcely the point at issue here: the question is what he would morally approve or find morally objectionable; and that, of course, may not be at all the same thing. If I commend, or adopt as right, some course of action which grossly damages the interests of another, you may point out to me, correctly no doubt, that I would not like it if my own interests were damaged in that way; there is, however, no reason why I should not admit this, and yet still maintain that, if our positions were reversed, that other person would be *right* to damage my interests exactly as I now propose to damage his. The ruthless landlord, for instance, on the point of ejecting his aged, ailing, and needy tenants into the snow, may concede not only that they will greatly dislike this treatment, but that he himself would dislike it no less if he were in their place; nevertheless, he may hold, it is right that they should be ejected, and that he himself should be ejected too, if he were in similar case. That he would not like it, he says, is neither here nor there; the point is that business is business, the economic show must go on. In order, that is, consistently to defend as unobjectionable my neglect of another's interests, I do not have to go to the somewhat unbalanced length of positively wanting my own interests to be neglected, or of somehow not disliking it when they are: all that I am required to do is to concede that neglect of my own interests by others would be unobjectionable. And there is nothing particularly strained or unbalanced about this; it is, for instance, the very essence of the gospel of self-help, of untrammelled competition in the old capitalist style — a gospel which, however morally disagreeable one may find it, has been consistently adopted by very many entirely sane men, and not only by those who have been winners in the jungle war. A man cannot, in effect, by the argument from universalisability, be constrained to attach *much* weight, if any, to the interests of others; for he may be entirely ready to concede that others are not morally required to attach much weight, if any, to his own, however intensely he may dislike it when, in the competitive free-for-all, it happens that he comes out on the losing side. But if this is true, the requirement of universalisability appears, whether in theory or in practice, to set almost no limit to the practical judgments which *can* be consistently made and maintained by sane men; and if so, it does not, as a weapon of moral argument, carry much fire-power.

Why then is Hare inclined to make such large claims for this real, but limited, dialectical weapon? Because (it is not, I think, unfair to say) his doctrine does not allow for genuine argument of any other kind. If asked to give reasons for some moral view I have expressed — that is, on this view, for some 'prescription' that I have issued — I may do one or both of two things: I may adduce certain facts about the case under consideration, or some principle, or principles, of which my presently-expressed view is an instance or application. But my principles, of course, are on this view themselves 'prescriptions' of mine; and such facts as I may adduce about the present case constitute *reasons* for my expressed view of it in so far as I have adopted, i.e. 'prescribed', some principle in accordance with which that view is derivable from those facts. Thus my giving of 'reasons' for my expressed prescription consists, on this view, essentially of my referring to and relying on *further* prescriptions of my own: what are reasons for me, are, for you, not only not necessarily good reasons, but possibly not reasons at all. And thus, what we speak of as argument between two parties emerges essentially as nothing more than the articulation by each of his own position. For you to say that my view is *wrong* is to say only that your position excludes that view; for me to 'argue' that my view is *right* is to show only that my position includes it. And there is nothing else, on this view, that argument can do; for there are no 'reasons' that either party can appeal to independently of, and so genuinely in support of, his own prescriptions. In this way it must inevitably appear to Hare that *real* argument can address itself only to the question of consistency; for so long as a man prescribes consistently, then on this view he has (since he has provided himself with) all the 'reasons' that any of his particular pronouncements may require;

46

and if I have 'reasons' for views that differ from his, he need claim only that my reasons are not reasons for him.[20]

It is, I believe, often not really noticed how surprising (at least) Hare's view of this question is. Most of us, no doubt, would agree readily enough that in moral matters we have to make up our own minds; we ourselves must decide on, embrace, commit ourselves to our moral standpoint. Further, we are probably ready enough to agree that moral discourse seems little susceptible of demonstrative argument; we have seldom much hope, in moral controversy, of confronting an opponent with a cogent proof of our views. Now it may seem that Hare is saying no more than this; but he is saying much more. For he is saying, not only that it is for us to decide what our moral opinions are, but also that it is for us to decide what to take as grounds for or against any moral opinion. We are not only, as it were, free to decide on the evidence, but also free to decide what evidence is. I do not, it seems, decide that flogging is wrong because I *am* against cruelty; rather, I decide that flogging is wrong because I *decide to be* against cruelty. And what, if I did make that decision, would be my ground for making it? That I am opposed to the deliberate infliction of pain? No — rather that I *decide to be* opposed to it. And so on. Now there are people, I think, whose moral views do seem to be formed and defended in this way — who, as one might say, not only make up their own minds, but also make up their own evidence; who pick and choose not only on the question what is right or wrong, but also on the question what are even to be admitted as relevant considerations. But such a person, surely, is not so much a model as a menace; not an exemplar of moral reasoning, but a total abstainer from any serious concern with reason. And if this really were a general feature of the human predicament, then to find cogent arguments in morals would not merely be difficult; it would be as hopeless as trying to play a competitive game in which each competitor was making up his own rules as he went along. All this is a matter to which we shall return in due course.

V. THE CONTENT OF MORALS

(i) PRACTICE AND PRINCIPLES

We turn now to a group of questions of a very different kind, though still concerned with, or arising out of, the question how moral discourse is related to conduct. These questions may be conveniently introduced by way of further, and this time more critical, consideration of the dictum, already quoted, from which Hare's argument begins: 'If we were to ask of a person "What are his moral principles?" the way in which we could be most sure of a true answer would be by studying what he *did*.'

I mentioned before that we should all, probably, be inclined *prima facie* to agree with this dictum; actions, after all, we think, do speak louder than words. But should we not now think more carefully about *what* actions tell us? Do they necessarily tell us what are a man's moral principles? One may think, not necessarily. For there seem on reflection to be at least two ways in which what a man does may fail to disclose his moral principles. First, may it not be the case that he has *no* moral principles? And second, may it not be the case that, though he has moral principles, he does not regularly act in accordance with the principles that he has? Let us examine these possibilities (if they *are* possibilities) further: they turn out to be a good deal more complex than one might have expected.

The first possibility — that the agent may have no moral principles — must, I think, be further subdivided. First, a man may have no principles of conduct at all; and second, he may have principles, but not *moral* principles. The former case does not seem particularly controversial; for surely no one would seek to deny that a man may, in the day-to-day conduct of his life, be so changeable, volatile, whimsical, and inconsistent that he could not be said to hold — and perhaps, for what it is worth, he does not even profess — any principles at all; his conduct composes no pattern, reveals no regularities, and *a fortiori* discloses no moral principles. But the latter case is decidedly more difficult. Might it be the case that, though a man consistently showed in his behaviour his adherence to certain principles, we should want to maintain that these were not *moral* principles?

Let us here consider, first, the case of a thorough-going egoist. He acts, let us suppose, always with deliberation, always has reasons for what he does, and is regularly guided by certain general principles of conduct. He is, however, never altruistic, nor even disinterested; even those of his actions which are agreeable, helpful, or advantageous to others are performed solely because he judges it to be in his own interests to perform them; his principles are all principles of self-regarding prudence. Now Hare, I believe, is required by his prescriptivism to hold that, in that case, those *are* his moral principles; at least if he does, as of course he may, 'prescribe' universally that any person should consider and pursue solely his own interests, then he has moral principles, namely, principles of egoism. This, however, may well be thought to be highly paradoxical. Many writers indeed, among whom may be mentioned Baier and Gauthier, have held that 'the moral point of view' involves, precisely and essentially, the *abandonment* of pure prudential egoism, and a readiness to consider as justifying grounds of action the interests or 'wants', ideally of everyone, but at any rate of at least some persons other than oneself.[21] To refuse to consider anything but one's own interests, they would hold, is precisely not to engage in moral thinking at all, but to be 'amoral'. Very similarly, it is the view of Nowell-Smith that the major point of moral principles is to promote 'social harmony';[22] and this is an end which the thorough-going egoist, even if he might regard it as likely to be advantageous on occasion, would not of course regard as particularly valuable in itself. He would not mind social chaos, so long as he himself was safely above the battle.

But there are other and perhaps more interesting possibilities here. May it not be the case that a man's conduct is guided principally, or even invariably, not by consideration of the interests of people in general, or even of his own, but rather by the pursuit of some *ideal* or system of ideals? And if so, might it not be the case that such an ideal was not necessarily a moral ideal, so that, here too, we might find an instance of conduct disclosing no moral principles?[23] Consider, for instance, the somewhat Nietzschean — or, for that matter, somewhat Greek — ideal of maximal development and large-scale, stylish exercise, of human capacities: the ideal, as it were, of the eminent and excellent specimen of humankind. Is this a *moral* ideal? Clearly this is not at all an easy question to answer. We may be inclined to say that this *is* a moral ideal, on the ground perhaps that it requires of its devotee at any rate much in the way of personal behaviour that we should all regard as morally admirable, and excludes much behaviour that we should all regard as morally bad. More importantly, we may think that any criterion of excellence in human conduct, if taken seriously enough, if felt as overridingly demanding and as involving remorse and self-reproach for failure to meet its demands, deserves, for the role that it may play in the life of its devotee, the accolade of morality. But on the other side we may note that — as, often, in the case of Nietzsche himself – this sort of ideal may be felt to be deeply antagonistic to 'morality', morality appearing by comparison to be repressive, cramping, timorous, even ignoble, an attempt by the feebler, more stifled specimens of humanity to fasten shackles on those more richly endowed than themselves. We may note that even the less ferocious ideals of Aristotle lead inevitably to the condemnation of the majority for defects which it would plainly be not in their power to remedy, and that the full realisation by some of his ideal conditions seems positively to require the attendant services of many more or less defective and humanly almost negligible subordinates. By contrast, would not 'the moral point of view' insist that a man is not to be condemned for failings or deficiencies for which he is not responsible? Are not all men, as moral beings, to be thought of as equal? If so, it may well seem more natural to regard, say, Nietzsche — as, of course, he from time to time regarded himself — not as propounding an unusual system of moral principles, but rather as abandoning moral attitudes altogether and as preaching, 'beyond good and evil', an ideal of conduct and character of a quite different kind.

It seems, then, somewhat contrary to the dictum we have before us, that there are grounds on which we might well wish to hold that, even if a man's conduct does disclose his adherence to principles, it does not necessarily apprise us of his *moral* principles, since the ruling principles of his conduct may not be moral principles at all. Consider now the not unrelated question whether a man might not simply fail to act consistently on the moral principles that he has. It is one of the more controversial implications of Hare's prescriptivism that this is *prima facie* impossible: for to 'accept a prescription' *is* to do what it says, and conversely, to fail to act in accordance with a principle *is* not to accept it. It has been urged against Hare on this point that his view is over-rigorous. It may be the case that a man who never, or hardly ever, acts as some principle requires cannot be regarded as sincere in his professions of subscription to the principle. But between total non-acceptance and unvarying compliance there are many intermediate cases: a man may act in breach of a principle in many different styles or manners, and may view his lapses with many different shades of regret, self-criticism, or remorse. Surely not every voluntary fall from virtue condemns every virtuous profession as insincere?[24]

But we should note here particularly the more fundamental point that Hare's view seems also tacitly to presuppose that moral principles must *necessarily* be of overriding authority. For to act in breach of a professed moral principle would not, of course, tend to put in question the sincerity of the agent unless it were assumed that his act could not be otherwise justified — that is, that there could be no conflicting considerations for the sake of which, while perfectly sincere in his profession of the moral principle, on this occasion he thinks it best not to act as that principle requires. If, on some occasion when I might have played cricket, I do not do so, you do not decide that I am insincere in professing to like playing cricket: for it is evident that I may have weightier grounds for not engaging, on this occasion, in that activity. But is it clear that moral principles may not sometimes be in similar case? Is it not clear on the contrary that, *if* there are tenable ideals which would not appropriately be regarded as moral ideals, a man might act for the sake of his ideal, quite consciously and deliberately, in breach of some moral principle which he quite sincerely professes? To say this, after all, is to say only that a man might regard considerations of some kind as more important than considerations of morality, and hence might take himself, on occasion, to be fully justified in not doing what he sincerely recognises to be right from the moral point of view. And to maintain that this is not a genuine possibility is, by implication, to make it a necessary truth that moral considerations are weightier, more important, than considerations of any other kind. But is it clear that this is in fact a necessary truth?

(ii) WHAT DOES 'MORAL' MEAN?

The question which is in effect raised by such reflections as these is really a very fundamental one, and it has been given, it seems to me, far less attention than it deserves. When philosophers discuss moral principles, moral judgment, moral discourse generally, *what* are they discussing? What does 'moral' mean? What distinguishes a moral view from views of other kinds? I think it must be quite clear that there is no easy answer to these questions; and yet, until they are answered, it seems that moral philosophers cannot really know what they are talking about, or at any rate, perhaps no less importantly, cannot be sure whether or not they are all talking about the same thing. It is, indeed, pretty clear that, historically, they have not been. Kant, for instance, takes it for granted that the 'moral law' imposes upon all rational beings unconditional, categorical demands to do and forbear — demands that are binding without any regard to human inclinations, purposes, desires, or interests, that have nothing essentially to do with human happiness, and call only for the absolute obedience of 'the good will'; his problem is to explain how there can be demands of that kind. But for Hume, for example, this problem does not arise at all. For it does not enter his head that there *are* any demands of that kind; on the contrary, he takes it entirely for granted that moral views give direct expression to human preferences and desires, and that it is the essence of a moral system to promote the interests, the general harmony and well-being, of human communities. That being so, it is of course entirely inevitable that their accounts of 'moral discourse' should be widely divergent; for it is not really the same thing that they are seeking to give an account of.

Now it is possible, I think, to distinguish at least four types of factors each of which has been taken, either alone or in conjunction with one or more of the others, as centrally characteristic of morality. First, it has occasionally been suggested that what is really distinctive of a moral view is, to put it somewhat crudely, the way in which those who take that view feel about it.[25] There is, it is said, a special sense of being *required* to act in a certain way, not by any external pressure or sanction, but rather by one's own consciousness of the sense of wrongdoing, of the guilt and self-reproach, that non-performance would incur. It is clear that there is not nothing in this; but it is perhaps equally clear that this can hardly be, by itself, a sufficient criterion of morality. It is not merely — though of course this is true — that a person may, for one reason or another, come to attach this psychological penumbra of guilt and self-reproach to performances, or non-performances, which are as a matter of fact entirely unobjectionable; for that is to say no more than that a person's moral feelings may sometimes be irrational. It is rather that a man may himself come to recognise that his sense of guilt and self-reproach is irrational and misplaced; and in that case, while the feelings may unfortunately prove very persistent, he presumably does not take their persistence as a ground for continuing to regard the issue, whatever it may be, as a moral one. It is possible, that is, as it were to detach one's feelings from the question whether some course of conduct is morally objectionable — to have the feelings appropriate to morally objectionable behaviour, and yet genuinely not to believe that one's behaviour is morally objectionable. But if so, then the occurrence or non-occurrence of certain feelings, the presence or absence of the characteristic sense of guilt, cannot be a sufficient criterion of a moral view.

Second, it has been held — less often, perhaps, explicitly than by implication — that, for any person, his moral principles and standards are to be identified as those which are in fact dominant in the conduct of his life. This is the view which is at least implicit in Hare's prescriptivism — 'A man's moral principles, in this sense, are those which, in the end, he accepts to guide his life by.' But this, as we mentioned before, looks highly paradoxical in this unqualified form. It is true, no doubt, that there are many good people whose lives are ultimately guided by their moral principles; but, on this view, we should be obliged to say that this was true, and even necessarily true, of everybody, or at least of everybody who has any principles at all; and surely that is wrong. Surely there have been individuals, and even whole societies, of whom or of which we should want to say that moral principles did not play any large part in their lives — that, perhaps, both their ideals of conduct and their actual conduct were shaped in accordance with standards that were not *moral* standards at all. Homer, in approving the ferocity, guile, and panache of the warrior chieftain, might be said to have been employing moral standards different from our own; but he might just as well, or better, be said not to have been employing moral standards at all.

We must, I think, regard as inadequate on just the same grounds the idea that a man's moral principles are *simply* those, whatever they may be, which he 'prescribes' for everyone alike; for surely we should wish to leave open the possibility of saying that some persons, and even some societies, though perhaps they 'prescribe' universally, nevertheless do not see things from 'the moral point of view'.

Finally, then, we may turn to the idea that morality should be somehow characterised, so to speak, by its subject-matter — the idea that what makes a view a *moral* view is, not the psychological penumbra by which it is surrounded, nor its predominance in the life of its proponent, but primarily its content, what it is about, the range or type of considerations on which it is founded.[26] The detailed working out of this idea, so far as any has been done, has taken various forms. It has been suggested, in the spirit of utilitarianism, that rules of morality are by definition those whose observance is at any rate believed to promote the 'greatest happiness', and whose violation is thought liable to increase the sum of human misery. Others have argued that we should seek the essence of morality, not in the notion of the promotion of happiness, but rather in that of the satisfaction of human needs, or of the reconciliation and promotion of human interests. Now it is surely hard to deny that there is very great plausibility in such views: for must it not surely be supposed, by anyone who claims to be propounding a moral principle, that observance of the principle he propounds would do some sort of *good*, and that breaches of it would do some sort of *harm*? If we ask a man why he holds the moral views that he expresses, must he not try to show, by way of justification, that the things he commends are in some sense or other *beneficial*, that the things he condemns are in some sense or other *damaging*? If he were to make no attempt to explain his position in such terms, what reason could there be for making, or for accepting, the supposition that the views in question were moral views?

(iii) HAS MORALITY A 'CONTENT'?

Let us now try, then, to survey our present problem from another angle. What does 'moral' mean? How are we to identify those principles which are moral principles, or to recognise that species of discourse which is moral discourse? We have just mentioned briefly — no doubt one could extend the list — four possible 'marks' of a moral view: its psychological penumbra; its actual importance in the individual's conduct of his life; its 'universalisability'; and its general topic — human happiness or interests, needs, wants, or desires. Now there is an important distinction to be found within the items on this list, and one that would continue to be of great importance however our somewhat sketchy list might be extended. This distinction is that between those 'marks' which do, and those which do not, assign to moral discourse a characteristic content, or subject-matter. In our short list, the first three items are thus distinguished from the fourth. For a view to which a certain psychological penumbra is attached may be a view *about* anything at all; and if a 'moral' view is to be thus identified, there will be nothing that morality, *ex officio*, so to speak, is about. Similarly, a principle which is actually dominant in the conduct of a life, or one which is 'prescribed universally' for all alike, may be a principle *about* anything at all; and if moral principles are to be thus identified, again there will be nothing that morality is essentially about. Our fourth item, however, is quite different in this respect; for by this 'mark' we shall identify as a moral view a view which is, in one way or another, *about* what is good or bad for people, what they want or need, what promotes or detracts from their happiness, well-being, or satisfaction; and if a moral view is to be *thus* identified, its psychological penumbra may be seen as an open question, and likewise the question whether a man who holds it is actually guided, or demands that others should be guided, predominantly by it in the actual conduct of life. The issue is this: which questions do we take to be answerable *a priori*? Is it true *a priori* that moral views predominate in the conduct of life, and a matter for investigation with what topics, in this instance or that, such views are concerned? Or is it true *a priori* that moral views are concerned with certain topics, and a matter for enquiry what role in life (or in discourse) such views, in this instance or that, may be found to play?

In this essay I cannot hope, and do not propose to try, to answer these questions, but only to call attention to what I take to be the urgent need for their further investigation. For it will be obvious that, for the purposes of moral theory, it is of the first importance that they should be answered — on the answer that is given to these questions will depend one's whole conception of what moral philosophy is called upon to do. Is it one's task to elucidate what one might call the formal character of moral discourse, its general character as a system of 'prescriptions', or 'evaluations'? Or is one to attempt to elucidate the *content* of morals, to describe in outline and to make distinctions within the general range of phenomena to which moral concepts are applicable? But the questions I have raised are important, I believe, not only for this reason; they are important, here and now, for the additional reason that recent moral philosophers have, often tacitly, answered them quite differently, and very seldom debated the question how they should be answered. Thus one sees moral theories which are not merely quite different, but actually aiming to do, in principle, quite different things; yet the difference of principle, I think, has been seldom recognised and, for that reason, scarcely ever discussed.

My own view (if it is worth expressing a view which one does not then try seriously to examine) is that morality *has* some at least roughly specifiable content. Looking again at our sketchy list of four possible 'marks' of a moral view, a moral judgment, a moral principle, the suggestion that I would myself be inclined to hazard is that while each is doubtless *relevant* to the characterisation of 'the moral', some form or other of the fourth is likely to turn out to be by far the most centrally important. It is probably true that there is, for very many people, a characteristic way of feeling about the rights and wrongs of conduct in certain cases, a way of feeling which goes with what they take to be moral issues; but apart from the possibility, mentioned above, that such feelings may occur in cases which even the subject himself does not seriously believe to involve moral issues, would one not be inclined also to say that a special way of feeling about certain issues is consequential upon, rather than definitive of, their character as *moral* issues? Rather similarly, it would seem to me more natural to say that, for very many people, certain principles play a predominant role in their own conduct, and are applied universally in judgment of the conduct of others, *because* they are believed to be moral principles, rather than, in reverse as it were, that their being moral principles *consists in* their being treated as overriding and of general application. On the other hand, it appears at least enormously plausible to say that one who professes to be making a moral judgment *must* at least profess that what is in issue is the good or harm, well-being or otherwise, of human beings — that what he regards as morally wrong is somehow damaging, and what he regards as morally right is somehow beneficial. There is no doubt at all that, apart from its high degree of vagueness, this would not be a sufficient characterisation of moral judgment; nevertheless it does appear to me to mention a feature which, in one way or another, any intelligible theory must recognise to be of central importance.[27]

There are, I think, four grounds at any rate on which this tentative suggestion might be resisted, and in conclusion of this section and in preparation for the next, these may be briefly considered. It might be said, first, that to define the concept of morality in any such terms would be to make moral attitudes reasonable by definition.[28] Would it not preclude us from regarding as moral at all codes of conduct, perhaps very barbarous and benighted, which so far from doing any good or promoting anyone's welfare, are in fact conducive to repression and cruelty? Yet we do wish to speak of barbarous and benighted moral codes. But this objection miscarries. For it would scarcely be suggested that a code of conduct, to be a moral code, must *be* such that its observance would satisfy anyone's needs or interests, or promote anyone's welfare; it is suggested only that it must be at least *supposed* to be so. Similarly, it is no doubt true that moral doctrines are often used, and often deliberately used, simply as instruments of repression or aggression, deliberately to do harm rather than good; but even so, it seems that, if it is to be even pretended that what is enforced is moral doctrine and that it is enforced for that reason, then it must also be at least pretended that some good is likely to be done thereby, or some harm prevented. Fear, or disgust, or envy, or resentment, or a mere taste for bullying, are very frequent causes of moral condemnation; but still, to give colour to the claim to moral concern, these causes must surely be veiled in some decent pretence of beneficent intentions.

Second, there arises a question that we have already glanced at. What about 'ideals'? Is it not possible for a man's life to be dominated, his conduct and his view of others' conduct determined at many points, not by consideration of his own or of others' needs or interests, of what is good or harmful for people in *that* sense, but by some ideal picture of how life should be lived, or of what is intrinsically noble, lofty, and admirable in human capacities and character? Of course this is possible, and a

most important actual determinant of human behaviour in some cases; it appears often as a concern, not for any specific advantage to be gained or good done by human activities, but rather for what one might call a certain style of activity, and for avoidance of what, while not harmful, is felt to be low, or unworthy, or disgraceful in itself. Now it has been argued by some that ideals of this type, 'pictures of life', must be included under the general concept of morality, not because they resemble more familiar moral concerns in topic or subject-matter, or are concerned with considerations of at all the same type, but simply because of the very similar role that they may play in conduct and the judgment of conduct; they bear similarly on the question 'how one should live'. It may be thought, however, as we earlier suggested, that one still can and should distinguish between those ideals that are, and those that are not, *moral* ideals. Surely it makes a great difference what kind of life devotion to an ideal would tend actually to involve, and what it proposes as grounds for respect or for condemnation. The ideals of the storm-trooper are, even confessedly, liable to be enormously destructive; those of the traditional gentleman are for the most part fairly harmless, and in some respects or in some situations may be highly advantageous. Is it not natural, and besides a perfectly defensible position, to reserve the appellation of *moral* ideals for those whose pursuit is supposed to tend actually to do good rather than harm, to make things on the whole better rather than worse, while regarding as not forming part of any 'moral point of view' such ideals as are openly destructive, or damaging, or pointless, or insane? No doubt it would be easy to think of many marginal cases; but then 'moral' is surely not, on any showing, a very exact word, or a word to be always very confidently applied or withheld.

Third, it might be urged by some that the enterprise of specifying an (even roughly) determinate content or subject-matter for morality must inevitably be vitiated by circularity. Hare has argued, for instance, against utilitarianism that the concept of happiness cannot be used to elucidate the concept of morality, if only for the reason that 'happiness' cannot be independently identified; we call a man happy not merely when we have, empirically, reason to think that his desires are adequately satisfied, but when we also approve in some degree of the desires he has.[29] Similarly, it might be urged that the notions of benefit or harm are themselves 'evaluative' notions — that they cannot be supposed to fix the content of morality for the reason that they themselves have no definite, independently specifiable content. And so for 'interests' or 'needs': a man's interests or needs cannot, surely, be the factual *grounds* of judgment, since it is a matter of judgment what his needs or his interests really are.

At this point we step, really, into a hornets' nest of problems; and once again we can here do little more than merely note that this is so. We must note first that the question crucially arises: how exactly *are* we to designate the considerations which, on this kind of view, are to be taken as fundamental to, and definitive of, moral discourse and moral judgment? Is it a question of what makes people happy? Or should we ask rather what avoids or diminishes unhappiness? Is it a matter simply of what people want, or must we bring in also the question what they really need? Should our attention be directed to human interests? And if so, does this topic coincide with, or does it not, the topic of what is of benefit to people or harms them? Obviously, not until such questions as these are first elucidated, and then answered, can we be in a position seriously to examine the question what *kind* of judgment is being proposed as fundamental to moral discourse, of what degree of certainty such judgments may be susceptible, and by what kind of investigation they would properly fall to be explored. Nevertheless, I believe it is defensible to hazard in advance the view that the charge of circularity, just mentioned, is not likely to prove effective. There are, I believe, two grounds for saying this. First, I believe that we all have, and should not let ourselves be bullied out of, the conviction that at least some questions as to what is good or bad for people, what is harmful or beneficial, are not in any serious sense matters of opinion. That it is a bad thing to be tortured or starved, humiliated or hurt, is not an opinion: it is a fact. That it is better for people to be loved and attended to, rather than hated or neglected, is again a plain fact, not a matter of opinion. We find here

no doubt a very wide penumbra of indeterminacy in which judgments must be made and may diverge, in which opinions and
attitudes may differ irreducibly: but who believes, except for bad
theoretical reasons, that there are no facts at all? But second —
and this perhaps is the sort of point which it will be felt less dis-
reputable for a philosopher to urge — the charge of circularity
will stand, *not* if the supposed fundamental content of morality
proves itself to be not independent of judgment and opinion, but
only if it can be shown itself to involve the exercise of *moral*
judgment. Those issues in terms of which morality is to be defined, if the definition is not to be merely circular, do not have
to be, without remainder, issues of absolutely neutrally deter-
minable fact: no more is required for theoretical purposes than
that they should not themselves be issues of moral judgment.
And surely it is reasonable to suppose that this condition is satisfied. That a certain person, or a certain community of persons,
would, if certain things were done, be in a better or worse condition, advantaged or disadvantaged, helped or harmed, may be
partly or even wholly a matter of judgment; but it is, I submit,
quite clear that it is not always, not wholly or necessarily, a matter
of *moral* judgment. But if so there is, from the point of view of
moral theory, no reason to object to the project of defining
morality at least partly in such terms.

We come, then, finally to the fourth and perhaps most notorious
objection of principle to the suggestion, however vaguely or
tentatively phrased, that moral judgment is concerned by definition or *ex officio*, in one way or another, with human good or harm,
needs, wants, interests, or happiness. Does not this suggestion
involve, it will be said, 'the Naturalistic Fallacy'? Does it not
offend against 'Hume's Law'?[30] For if this suggestion were
accepted, it would seem that facts of certain kinds about the
world — namely, facts about people's needs or interests, happiness or wants — might in principle *entail* a particular moral
judgment. But this, it has been held, is manifestly wrong in principle: if anything is clear, it is that 'naturalism' is untenable. This
is a matter that calls for more extended consideration.

VI. NATURALISM

(i) THE ANTI-NATURALIST THESIS

In this closing section, I shall not seek to show that 'naturalism' is true; for that purpose, it is not clear enough what naturalism is supposed to be. Part of the reason for this is that there do not appear actually to be any self-confessed naturalists among moral philosophers; and the untenability of naturalism has seemed, at least until quite recently, so very evident that its critics have not thought it worth while to set out in great detail the doctrine they have so regularly rejected. Accordingly I think that the most profitable proceeding will be briefly to review some characteristic *anti*-naturalistic tenets, and to consider what follows from those, if any, which seem to be sound.

As we noted at a much earlier stage, the expression 'the naturalistic fallacy' was introduced by G. E. Moore in his *Principia Ethica*, though the idea is certainly older than that, and has commonly been supposed to originate with Hume. We need not spend time, however, on Moore's exposition of the anti-naturalist case, which has been generally recognised — by Moore himself among others — as unsatisfactory. To commit the naturalistic fallacy, according to Moore, is to make two mistakes — first, that of offering a definition of a quality which is indefinable, and second, that of offering a definition of a non-natural quality in terms of natural qualities. But these mistakes are not, in fact, necessarily connected; and it would seem that the expression 'the *naturalistic* fallacy' might appropriately be reserved to designate the second of them. Here, then, Moore is alleging, first, that 'ethical qualities' are non-natural, and second, that non-natural qualities are not definable in terms of natural ones. The trouble is that he scarcely does more than barely allege this; he does not satisfactorily explain the terms 'natural' and 'non-natural', or seek to show why qualities of the one kind are not definable in terms of those of the other kind; so that there is really nothing here for critical discussion to take hold of.

We may also dismiss with a certain briskness one more modern-looking view which has sometimes been offered as an elucidation of, or amendment to, Moore's doctrine. This is the view that 'evaluative' expressions are not definable in terms of 'descriptive' expressions. The trouble here is that there do not exist the two distinct classes of expressions ostensibly referred to. It is possible, no doubt, to distinguish evaluating from describing — for example, describing Jenkins's performance of a flute sonata, from evaluating his performance. But it is not, in general, possible to make this distinction merely on the basis of the expressions used; for it is probably true to say that any expression which occurs in the context of the evaluation of something could also occur in the context of the description of something, and vice versa — this distinction is simply not a distinction of *vocabulary*. Thus, if 'evaluative expression' means 'expression used in evaluating something', and 'descriptive expression' means 'expression used in describing something', the position will be that most, perhaps all, evaluative expressions are *also* descriptive expressions, and vice versa; so that the view mentioned above turns out to be the merest nonsense.

Criticism of this view, though, suggests a possible amendment of it. Perhaps the real point at issue — the point which, it might be suggested, was really at the back of Moore's mind — is that *evaluation* is not reducible to *description*; that there is an insurmountable difference of principle between the activities of evaluating something and describing it, between just 'stating the facts' and passing any sort of judgment upon them. There is almost certainly some good sense in which this would be true; though one must not, indeed, suppose the distinction to be a clear and sharp one in ordinary discourse.[31] In legal proceedings, for instance, comparable distinctions are formally brought out and observed with some care — the business of giving evidence, say, is clearly distinguished from that of presenting a case, and both are clearly distinguished from the business of giving judgment: at any stage there is a perfectly clear and determinate answer to the question which, if any, of these activities is then going on. But ordinary discourse is not, since it does not need to be, similarly regimented; if I am telling someone, for instance, about the career of Mussolini, it would be unrealistic to look for — to assume that there must be — a point at which description of his doings terminates, and evaluation of them begins; 'talking about' Mussolini in an ordinary conversational manner is most unlikely to be thus susceptible of decomposition into sharply distinct ingredients. However, although this distinction is not always to be found, it is probably true to say that it could always be made; the instruction 'First *describe* Mussolini's career, and then *evaluate* it' is a more or less intelligible instruction, and one has some notion of how it might be obeyed. That there is, then, a difference of some sort between evaluating and describing seems to be true, and of course is quite naturally to be expected.

I think it is clear, however, that the anti-naturalist philosopher is contending for something much more than this unambitious truism. What seems to be suggested is, not merely that description and evaluation are different, but that they are in an important sense *independent*. No description, it is said, ever *commits* us to any particular evaluation; any description might be accepted, and any evaluation rejected, without logical inconsistency. Now of most ordinary discourse this suggestion is probably false. Since, as we have just said, there are in ordinary discourse comparatively few regimented distinctions between one speech-activity and another, one might expect to find description and evaluation so inextricably intermingled as to constitute, as it were, a seamless garment; and there cannot be logically independent parts of a tract of discourse which has, in the required sense, no distinguishable parts. But perhaps this does not matter: perhaps all that the anti-naturalist thesis requires is that, though we often do not, we always *could* so 'state the facts' of any case that evaluation of that case would be a logically independent operation. It might be at least possible, for instance, to describe the career of Mussolini in such terms that, given that description, any *evaluation* of his career might be accepted or rejected without logical error.

Why is this so? The suggestion, I believe, could be formulated as follows. Evaluation of any kind, it would be said, whether of people or objects or actions or anything else, implies the acceptance of, and must be done in the light of, certain standards, rules, principles, or criteria of judgment. If, for instance, candidates are to be graded in an examination, certain features of possible performances in that examination must be accepted as *criteria* for the assignment of grades — this might be, in a very simple case, simply the number of problems solved, or right answers given. Now no one, it is suggested, is ever *logically* obliged to accept any given feature *as* a standard or criterion, or any general proposition *as* a rule or principle of judgment. While agreeing that, for example, the performance of a certain candidate does in fact have a certain feature, that it can be correctly described in that way, one may refuse to accept that feature as a criterion of merit, and so decline to *evaluate* the performance on that basis, or at all. There can be description, but no evaluation, without the adoption or recognition of standards; but if so, since one cannot be logically obliged to adopt any particular facts or features, or even any at all, *as* standards for favourable or unfavourable judgment, the specification of facts or features in a description cannot *logically* lead to any particular evaluation, or even any at all. One may concede the presence of the features specified, or admit the facts, but not adopt or recognise those features or facts as having the status of criteria, or standards, or principles, or rules.

It would no doubt be possible to object to this formulation of the anti-naturalist thesis as over-simplified and excessively schematic. The actual business of evaluation, it might be insisted, is very often both far more complicated, and also far less clearcut, than is suggested by this simple picture of assigning definite grades by reference to definite standards. Do we always know exactly what the relevant standards, criteria, or principles are? Can we always be certain what does or does not satisfy them, or specify exactly on the basis of *what* facts or features we make the judgments we do? Again, in what sense if any is it true to say that 'stating the facts' is independent of the use or recognition of standards? I shall not, however, on this occasion object to the thesis outlined above on such grounds; for it is in any case, I believe, far less interesting and important than has often been supposed. Its importance for, in particular, moral philosophy has been thought to consist in certain of its implications; but it does not really have, as I shall try to show, those particular implications which have been thought to be important.

(ii) WHAT THE THESIS DOES AND DOES NOT IMPLY

First, I believe that the temptation has not always been resisted to dramatise the anti-naturalist thesis, as it were, by turning it round. Suppose that we agree that no one is ever logically obliged to accept any given feature as a criterion of merit; it has perhaps been tempting to see in this the further implication that absolutely anything *might* be regarded as a criterion of merit. But this is fallacious. That no one is obliged to eat any particular kind of substance as food does not imply that absolutely any kind of substance might be eaten as food. But not only is the inference fallacious; its conclusion is surely false. For to adopt some feature as a criterion of merit is to imply, in some way appropriate to the particular context, some preference for what has that feature over what does not have it; and to prefer what has that feature is, in some way way appropriate to the particular context, to want, or to want there to be, what has that feature, and to want it *because* it has that feature. Now there are, perhaps, no logical limits to what a person may be said to want; and doubtless there is nothing of which it can be said that necessarily everyone wants it; but are there not limits, nevertheless, to what a person may be said *understandably* to want? What does he want it for? What appeals to him about it? In what way, should he get what he wants, does he expect to be satisfied? If we have no notion at all of answers to these questions, then someone's assertion that he wants whatever it may be is, in a clear sense, not intelligible to us; we do not understand what he says, because we do not understand *him*. How would beings from Mars, if set down, say, in London, evaluate what they found there? What would they be favourably struck by, what would they take against? Clearly one has no way of answering these questions, precisely because one knows nothing about such beings; one does not know what their needs would be, what they would want of their environment, what they would like or dislike. Thus, though in a sense one might say that absolutely any feature of their environment might be regarded by them as a criterion of merit or desirability, this is not to say that we could always *understand* its being so regarded; it is rather to concede that we have no understanding of the evaluations of hypothetical Martians. Conversely, a feature, to function as an intelligible criterion of desirability or merit, must surely be such that we could at least understand, say, someone's wanting something to have it; and it is not true that just any feature at all meets this condition. It follows further that it is not true to say, as has been said, that evaluation rests ultimately on *choice*. For we do not choose to want this or that, to prefer one thing to another; when we have choices to make, we do not in turn choose what are to be reasons for choosing. To take that line, as we suggested earlier that prescriptivism does, is to imply that in the end there *are* no reasons at all.

The 'independence' of description and evaluation, then, does not imply, nor is it the case that, just anything can function as an (intelligible) criterion of evaluation. But now, is it not even more plainly the case that not just anything can function as a criterion of *moral* evaluation? This is not the place to attempt the considerable task of determining what the limits here exactly are; but that there *are* such limits seems to me perfectly evident.[32] Could we say, perhaps, vaguely enough for present purposes, and glancing back to certain points urged in the preceding section, that the limits are set somewhere within the general area of concern with the welfare of human beings? To say this is not, indeed, to say very much; but it is not to say nothing. For it is to say, in fact, at least this: that the *relevance* of considerations as to the welfare of human beings *cannot*, in the context of moral debate, be denied. (Again, of course, we do not *choose* that this should be so; it *is* so, simply because of what 'moral' means.) It will be obvious, I imagine, that to say this does not run counter to the 'independence'-thesis. For what that thesis says is that no one is logically obliged to accept any given feature as a criterion of merit; and if we say, as in effect we have just done, that certain features must necessarily be accepted as criteria of *moral* merit, we can and must go on at once to concede that no one, of course, is obliged by logic to engage in moral judgment or debate. That there are, as it were, necessary criteria of moral value does not imply that anyone, let alone everyone, necessarily evaluates things with reference to those criteria; it is only that we *must* do so *if* we are prepared, as we may not be, to consider the question 'from the moral point of view'.

What this amounts to is the proposition that the anti-naturalist thesis as formulated above, while probably true, has really no great importance for moral philosophy. It is a thesis, as one might put it, about the 'general theory' of evaluation: and it says, probably quite correctly about evaluation in general, first, that that activity presupposes standards; and second, that there are, so to speak, no necessary or 'built-in' standards of evaluation that must (logically) be adopted by anyone who accepts or offers a particular description of the world. But this, as I hope is now plain, does not imply that there are no necessary standards of *moral* evaluation; for it may be the case, as I am tentatively suggesting it is, that certain standards — that is, the *relevance* at least of a certain particular range of considerations — though they do not have to be accepted at all, must be accepted *if* the claim to be evaluating *morally* is to be seriously made. Thus I suggest that we may concede to the anti-naturalist the (from the point of view of moral philosophy) uninteresting point that evaluation in general is, in the sense explained, independent of description, and then proceed to the interesting business of investigating moral evaluation in particular — enquiring, that is, what it is to appraise things 'from the moral point of view', and what in particular that range of considerations is whose relevance is implicit in the adoption of that point of view. If to be a 'naturalist' is to maintain that certain kinds of facts or features are necessarily relevant criteria of moral evaluation, then I would surmise that 'naturalism' is true. If the anti-naturalist then maintains that there are no critieria of evaluation which anyone is logically obliged to accept, then I believe that 'anti-naturalism' is also true. But one should doubtless conclude that, on this showing, the terminology of 'naturalism' and 'anti-naturalism' is somewhat infelicitous, since the two expressions designate views which are perfectly compatible with one another. One might say that it is proper to be a naturalist in *ethics*, an anti-naturalist in what we have called the 'general theory' of evaluation: but it would probably be preferable simply to retire both expressions from further philosophical employment, and to investigate the actual position without benefit of labels.

(iii) A FINAL NOTE ABOUT MORAL ARGUMENTS

It will probably be objected against the position we have now tentatively reached — that, notwithstanding the general 'anti-naturalist' doctrine, there are certain kinds of facts or features which are necessarily criteria of *moral* evaluation — that this implies that moral arguments might in principle be demonstrative, logically cogent. The position we have reached does, I think, have this implication; but I see no reason why we should be alarmed by that. For one thing, it seems clear that really demonstrative reasoning in morals is certain to be in fact exceedingly rare. There seem to be at least five reasons why this must be so. First, while the (necessarily relevant) notion of 'the welfare' of human beings surely has, as one might put it, a perfectly clear and determinate core or centre, no one would wish to deny that it has also an extensive penumbral fringe of vagueness and indeterminacy; there is room for much diversity of opinion as to what *constitutes* 'the welfare' of human beings, not indeed at all points, but still at many points. Second, in considering, say, the moral rights and wrongs of a proposed course of action, it is often necessary to 'weigh' short-term good or harm against long-term harm or good; and such metaphorical 'weighing', though of course not impossible, is not susceptible of great exactness. Third, there will usually be need for similarly inexact 'weighing' of good or harm to some individuals against harm or good to others; and fourth, it will often be necessary to strike

69

a metaphorical 'balance' between the good *and* harm that would accrue to single individuals. And if we add, fifth, the fairly obvious fact that the information relevant to solution of a moral problem — conspicuously, information about the future course of events — will very often not be obtainable with any high degree of certainty, then we shall see how extremely uncommon it must be, in fact, for moral reasoning to lead *indisputably* to just one particular conclusion. One could argue conclusively that some course of action would be, say, morally wrong if one could show that that course of action would lead *quite certainly* to certain consequences, which would constitute *indisputably* some serious harm to some innocent person or persons, and that there would accrue *quite certainly* no good to anyone which could *possibly* be held to outweigh those harmful consequences. It is not that there are no cases which satisfy these conditions; it could be shown, for instance, with this sort of conclusiveness that it would be morally wrong for me to induce in my children addiction to heroin. But, of course, when *all* the relevant considerations point *indisputably* one way, it is unlikely to occur to anyone that the argument is worth stating; the question, in fact, is scarcely likely ever to be raised. Nevertheless, that such an argument, if stated, could be really demonstrative, seems to me clear; and anyone who, if such an argument is put to him, denies that the conclusion follows — who holds, while conceding the facts, that, for instance, it would *not* be morally wrong for me to induce in my children addiction to heroin — shows either that he has not really followed the argument, or that he does not know what 'morally wrong' means. It is perfectly consistent with this to admit, as of course one must, that *serious* moral disagreements — arising, that is, on matters about which some people actually do disagree — are exceedingly unlikely to be capable of being conclusively resolved, to the satisfaction of all parties, by any argument whatever.

Some may still feel that the idea that moral arguments can in principle be demonstrative must be resisted, on the ground that one cannot after all make people morally virtuous by argument. But this is a mere confusion. For even the best of argu-

ments, of course, is not 'cogent' in the way that, say, a police-
man may be; it cannot prevent people from behaving badly, or
make them behave well; but that is not to say that it may not be
a demonstrative argument. For even though some moral argument be entirely demonstrative, no one has to accept its conclusion as a basis for action. One may, obviously, simply neglect
the conclusion, and proceed to act without reference to moral
considerations. One may not care, or one may think other things
to be of greater importance. Even if I show you conclusively
that your course of action is morally wrong, and even if you
clearly see and admit that to be so, you may still be entirely *unmoved* by the argument I give you.

What then, one may ask, is the value of argument in moral
matters? If, even in those rare cases in which the argument is
conclusive and the conclusion accepted without any question,
the wrong thing may nevertheless be *done*, why is it worth de-
ploying moral argument at all? But of course the answer to this
question is very obvious. It is that those considerations to which,
as I have suggested, moral reasoning necessarily appeals are considerations by which, as a matter of brute fact, most people are
not entirely unmoved. Those considerations of good or harm
to people which, I have suggested vaguely enough, figure
analytically in setting moral standards and moral principles,
and which provide accordingly the basis for the pros and cons of
moral argument, are matters which most people in some degree
do actually care about. (They do not *choose* to do so; they *do*.)
Certainly not many people are nice enough to be *very* much concerned about these matters; nor intelligent enough to be concerned about them intelligently; nor rational enough to be actually motivated by intelligent concern. Nevertheless, if it were not
the case that there existed a certain range of considerations, having to do in general with the welfare of human beings, about
which most people cared very much some of the time, and cared
to some extent much of the time, then not only would moral
argument, however conclusive, be pointless and ineffective;
moral discourse would simply not occur. That there is, as we all
know there is, a very widespread, though of course not complete,

consensus as to what is desirable and undesirable in human affairs is a condition of the existence of a common moral vocabulary; and just the same condition gives us a reason for supposing that moral judgment and moral discussion are not pointless, because not always ineffective, activities. That moral argument is not more effective than we find it to be is probably attributable to the cross that all arguments have to bear: an argument offers reasons to people, and people are not always reasonable.

VII. PROSPECT

These closing pages, no doubt, would be properly the place for a conclusion; but I think it will be clear to anyone who has read so far that no conclusion has been reached but rather, as I would hope, a starting-point for new enquiries. I will try, therefore, briefly to recapitulate my discontents about the way things have been going in recent ethical theory, and to suggest what the chief questions are that seem to me to be outstanding.

First of all, I would insist that we must start from the recognition that there is something peculiarly puzzling and problematic, peculiarly *arguable*, about the whole phenomenon of morals. Not everyone, naturally, feels this, but even if one does not feel it the record shows it to be so. So much is unclear; so many different views have been taken — and not only, of course, about what is morally right or wrong, but about *what it is to be* morally right or wrong. How are moral problems to be distinguished from those that are not moral? How, when one meets a moral issue, does one recognise it as such? How important, among the various and conflicting considerations which bear from time to time on the conduct of human lives, is the place that moral considerations have, or should have? And why? Have there been, or could there be, quite ordinary people who had no moral views at all, to whom morality meant nothing? What is the ground, or are the grounds, on which rests the consciousness of moral distinctions? How do we, how should we, how far can we sensibly hope to, resolve or diminish moral disagreements by discussion and argument? What goes wrong, what is the penalty, if moral rules are neglected or broken? All these are quite certainly matters on which there are and have been, not only among philosophers, widely diverse opinions, and shifting, confused opinions: there is no set of answers which has any claim to be *obviously* correct.

And this is why 'intuitionism' is completely unhelpful. For all these questions, on that view, are pronounced undiscussable: we are told that there is something to be 'seen', but nothing to be said: it is all too obvious for words. But this is not true, and it seems extraordinary that it should ever have been believed.

'Emotivism' is not really very helpful either. This doctrine has hold, indeed, of one very broad truth — the truth, not wildly exciting but still sometimes neglected, that the institution and apparatus of morality have a practical point; what the whole thing is *for* is the promotion of certain kinds of conduct and states of affairs, and the diminution of the incidence of others. But the doctrine not only fails completely to distinguish the ways in which, in morals, this point is pursued from other ways; more damagingly, it positively mis-assimilates those ways to those of such purely manipulative procedures as propaganda, emotional bullying, brain-washing, and the hard sell. We ask how moral discourse is different; we are told that it is not.

The case of 'prescriptivism' is more complex and more interesting. There is retained in this body of doctrine the truth that the institution of morality has a practical point, and there is added the further truth that, in morals, this point is not pursued merely by the exertion of causally efficacious influences. Morality is for rational beings, treated *as* rational. But that moral discourse is a form of 'prescriptive' discourse is a thesis which, while seductively truistic in one sense, is fatally impoverishing in another. In so far as the thesis is that moral discourse is in some way essentially (and not just causally) related to conduct, it is a completely impregnable platitude; but in so far as it attempts a serious assimilation of all moral judgments to imperatives, it seems to leave us once more with practically nothing to discuss. There is nothing to be discovered, but only choices to be made; no reasoning can possibly be conclusive, for choices may differ; the scope of morality cannot be determined, for we cannot set limits to the choices that a man might make. The importance of morality is not a genuine question, since what predominantly guides a man's decisions *is* morality for him. There is nothing either right or wrong but choosing makes it so. What seems objectionable is not so much that these implications are false (although, as a matter of fact, I think they are); it is rather that they seem to sidetrack all serious discussion. The innocent-looking thesis that moral discourse is 'prescriptive' discourse seems, almost miraculously, to bring in its train a string of dusty answers to large and complicated questions which, while saying almost nothing, seem to leave nothing further to be said. Perhaps we do not know that this is wrong; but it is more important that, at present, we certainly do not know that it is right.

What is to be done, then? One thing that, in my view, is of the first importance is that we should begin more nearly at the beginning than is commonly done, and determine how we propose that the subject-matter is to be identified. When we talk about 'morals' we do *not* all know what we mean; what moral problems, moral principles, moral judgments are is *not* a matter so clear that it can be passed over as a simple datum. We must discover when we would say, and when we would not, that an issue is a moral issue, and why: and if, as is more than likely, disagreements should come to light even at this stage, we could at least discriminate and investigate what reasonably tenable alternative positions there may be. This surely would not be, as some philosophers have implied, a boringly 'verbal' investigation of the word 'moral'; for if we do not investigate the sense and scope of this word, how do we know what the phenomena are which moral theory is to deal with? To be uninterested in the *word* is to be uninterested in the subject — in what it is that distinguishes this particular subject from others. It may be the case that this subject is *not* distinguished in any sharp way from others that concern the appraisal of character and conduct; but if that is so, at least we shall do well to appreciate that, and why, it is so. Distinctions do not have to be sharp to be worth taking note of.

Investigation of the sense and scope of 'moral' is desirable not only because it seems prudent that, in moral theory, we should decide what we are talking about. It is also possible that such investigation should show what the basis is for making moral distinctions — that is, what class or range of considerations, identifying an issue as a moral issue, are consequentially relevant to moral assesssment of it. This *might* not be so, since it is in principle possible that the sense of 'moral' should be found to leave its range of application completely indeterminate. But that seems to me unlikely: and *if* we can properly attach the word to any even roughly determinate range of phenomena, then many further questions will come up for consideration. If we know on what basis, with an eye to what, moral distinctions are made, we can usefully consider, for example, why some would hold — and also, doubtless, why others would deny — that such distinctions are of unique importance, and uniquely authoritative in issues of practical judgment; this question, an answer to which seems usually to be assumed, would become susceptible of serious examination. And then — if we know what the basis of distinction is here, and what 'weight' attaches, and why, to the distinctions made — we may be able usefully to consider what the prospects are for the fruitfulness of moral discussion. We can consider how far disputants could, and how far they could not, properly differ in what they take to be relevant to matters at issue; how far they could, and how far they could not, properly differ in their 'weighing' of those factors they take to be relevant. This matter needs to be discussed in substance, not in form; for there is nothing formally peculiar in, or distinctive of, argument in morals; if there are special features here, as quite probably there are, I would suppose them to be founded in what argument in morals is *about*. If such arguments are, as philosophers seem usually to conclude, liable to be peculiarly indecisive, this is not because of any formal deficiencies or oddities, but because the subject-matter is some-how recalcitrant to exact, 'objective', appraisal. When we know what the subject-matter is, we shall be better placed to see why, and how far, this is the case.

It is perhaps rather late to apologise for overstating my case; but I am not quite unconscious, here and there, of having done so. In suggesting as I have done that much recent moral theory has been misguided in its aims and unrewarding in its results, I have not put in the qualifications, points on the other side, which strict justice would require but limitations of space do not allow. Of course, from recent and contemporary moral philosophers there is much to be learned and much profit to be derived. Nevertheless, this is a subject in which there is still almost everything to be done.

NOTES

1. The terminology here is J. L. Austin's, and is explained in his *How to Do Things with Words* (1962), pp. 94 ff. Briefly and roughly, the distinction Austin has in mind is that between *what is done by* saying something, e.g. getting a person to go away, and *what is done in* saying something, e.g. ordering him to go away. *What is said*, of course, is distinguishable from both of these.

2. *Principia Ethica* (1903), p. 6.

3. *Principia Ethica*, p. 162.

4. See, for example, J. M. Keynes, 'My Early Beliefs', in *Two Memoirs* (1949); and Leonard Woolf, *Sowing* (1961).

5. *Mind*, 1912; reprinted in *Moral Obligation* (1949), pp. 1–17.

6. *Moral Obligation*, pp. 16–17.

7. See, for example, *The Right and the Good* (1930), chap. ii, and *Foundations of Ethics* (1939), pp. 83–84.

8. R. Carnap, *Philosophy and Logical Syntax* (1935), p. 24.

9. M. Schlick, *Problems of Ethics* (1939), particularly chap. i.

10. For an excellent short account of Stevenson's view, see his 'The Emotive Meaning of Ethical Terms', *Mind*, 1937: reprinted in *Logical Positivism*, ed. Ayer (1959).

11. *Logical Positivism*, p. 269.

12. On this point see Hare's admirable paper in the symposium 'The Freedom of the Will', *Proceedings of the Aristotelian Society*, Supplementary volume xxv, 1951.

13. On this distinction, see Austin, *How to Do Things With Words*, particularly Lecture x.

14. Stevenson, in *Logical Positivism*, p. 280.

15. *Freedom and Reason* (1963), p. 4.

16. 'The study of imperatives is by far the best introduction to ethics.' *The Language of Morals* (1952), p. 2.

17. *The Language of Morals*, p. 1.

18. P. H. Nowell-Smith, *Ethics* (1954), p. 98.

19. On this point see particularly *Freedom and Reason*, part ii.

20. Cf. Philippa Foot's very able article 'Moral Arguments', *Mind*, 1958.

21. K. Baier, *The Moral Point of View* (1958), and D. P. Gauthier, *Practical Reasoning* (1963).

22. *Ethics* (1954), p. 229.

23. See *Freedom and Reason*, particularly chap. 8; and P. F. Strawson, 'Social Morality and Individual Ideal', *Philosophy*, 1961. There are relevant observations also in Stuart Hampshire's *Thought and Action* (1959), particularly pp. 249 ff.

24. See P. L. Gardiner, 'On assenting to a moral principle', *Proceedings of the Aristotelian Society*, 1954–5.

25. I take some view of this nature to be implied by J. Bennett in his critical discussion (*Mind*, 1965) of Gauthier's *Practical Reasoning*.

26. This is a view, of course, which has never lacked defenders. Among recent writers I think one might assign Nowell-Smith, Toulmin, Baier, Gauthier, and (most clearly) Mrs. Foot to this camp — not that they all say the same thing, but that they see the same *kind* of thing as needing to be said.

27. It might be objected that, in suggesting that a concern with human benefit or harm is essential to anything deserving the name of a moral view, one is illicitly incorporating some kind of utilitarian 'humanism' into the very definition of morality. Would not this suggestion be indignantly repudiated by, for instance, the religious believer, for whom the foundation of morality is the Word of God? But I am inclined to think that such an objection would be unsound. For I suspect that religious views differ from 'humanist' views, not by denying the essential moral relevance of human benefit or harm, but rather by incorporating very different beliefs as to what really is good or bad for human beings. The religious believer finds in a supernatural order a whole extra dimension of pre-eminently important gains and losses, benefits and harm; his difference with the non-believer is not on the question whether these are of moral significance, but simply on the question whether they are real or chimerical. He might also wish to expand what might be called the moral population to include moral beings supposed not to be human; but to this, if there are such beings, no one surely will object.

28. See H. L. A. Hart, *The Concept of Law* (1961), p. 177.

29. *Freedom and Reason*, pp. 125–9.

30. 'Hume's Law ("No 'ought' from an 'is'"), to which I have repeatedly declared my adherence.' Hare, *Freedom and Reason*, p. 108.

31. Cf. Toulmin and Baier, 'On Describing', *Mind*, 1952.

32. The case has been excellently discussed by Philippa Foot, in 'Moral Beliefs', *Proceedings of the Aristotelian Society*, 1958–9.

BIBLIOGRAPHY

(Arranged in order of publication, except where more than one book has been listed for a single author.)

Moore, G. E., *Principia Ethica* (Cambridge University Press, 1903).

Ross, W. D., *The Right and the Good* (Oxford: Clarendon Press, 1930).

Foundations of Ethics (Oxford: Clarendon Press, 1939).

Ayer, A. J., *Language, Truth, and Logic* (Gollancz, 1936).

Stevenson, C. L., *Ethics and Language* (Yale University Press, 1944).

Prichard, H. A., *Moral Obligation* (Oxford: Clarendon Press, 1949).

Prior, A. N., *Logic and the Basis of Ethics* (Oxford: Clarendon Press, 1949).

Toulmin, S. E., *An Examination of the Place of Reason in Ethics* (Cambridge University Press, 1950).

Broad, C. D., *Ethics and the History of Philosophy* (Routledge & Kegan Paul, 1952).

Hare, R. M., *The Language of Morals* (Oxford: Clarendon Press, 1952).

Freedom and Reason (Oxford: Clarendon Press, 1963).

Nowell-Smith, P. H., *Ethics* (Penguin Books, 1954; Blackwell (hard-cover), 1957).

Baier, K., *The Moral Point of View* (Cornell University Press, 1958).

Montefiore, A. C., *A Modern Introduction to Moral Philosophy* (Routledge & Kegan Paul, 1958).

Hampshire, S., *Thought and Action* (Chatto & Windus, 1959).

Warnock, M., *Ethics since 1900* (Home University Library, 1960).

Hart, H. L. A., *The Concept of Law* (Oxford: Clarendon Press, 1961).

Austin, J. L., *How do Do Things with Words* (Oxford: Clarendon Press, 1962).

Edel, A., *Method in Ethical Theory* (Routledge & Kegan Paul, 1963).

Gauthier, D. P., *Practical Reasoning* (Oxford: Clarendon Press, 1963).

A useful collection of readings is W. S. Sellars and J. Hospers eds.), *Readings in Ethical Theory* (Appleton-Century-Crofts, 1952).

Printed in Great Britain by
Richard Clay (The Chaucer Press), Ltd.,
Bungay, Suffolk